AMERICAN HISTORY
A Geek's Guide

AMERICAN HISTORY

A Geek's Guide

Douglas B. Lyons

BARNES
& NOBLE

NEW YORK

This 2007 edition published by Barnes & Noble, Inc. by arrangement with MQ Publications Limited.

ISBN-13: 978-0-7607-8996-4
ISBN-10: 0-7607-8996-7

1 3 5 7 9 10 8 6 4 2

Printed in Korea

Contents

FOREWORD
DOUGLAS B. LYONS

The hardest part about writing this book has not been what to include. There is plenty to include. It has been deciding what *not* to include. Lesley Gore sang: "IT'S MY PARTY, AND I'LL CRY IF I WANT TO." That's my creed here too: It's my book, and I'll include what I want to, and I'll exclude what I want to. When you write *your* book, *you* have the same artistic license.

So if you'd like an explanation of the XYZ Affair, you won't find it here. I just don't think it seems important any more. Like Quemoy and Matsu, whose fate was a key difference between candidates Nixon and Kennedy in the 1960 election. How about the gold versus silver issue in the campaign of 1896? Doesn't seem important any more—to me. (But I still have a few "William Jennings Bryan for president" buttons, showing the hands of a clock at sixteen to one.) I have not included the Great Locomotive Chase, the Donner Party, the Haymarket Riot, or everybody's favorite American eccentric, the Emperor Norton—although I enjoy reading about them. That's not my test. Relevance and importance— that's what I think merits inclusion. That's why the entry for the Scopes trial is so long. It's still important.

I have given short shrift to the gunfight at the O.K. Corral, and made scant mention of Jamestown. The entries would have to be too long. No letters of complaint about things that were omitted, please. I know. I just cannot include everything.

Do I have to include events that happened in other countries? I included Bob Beamon's long jump record at the 1968 Olympics in Mexico City, but not Mark Spitz's seven gold medals at Munich in 1972. I'd have to explain about the Arab terrorist attack on Israeli athletes, Spitz (who is Jewish) being spirited away from the games…It's already too long.

This book has very few entries on America's wars: the French and Indian Wars, the Mexican War, the Revolutionary War, The Blackhawk War, in which Lincoln served, Shay's Rebellion, the War of 1812, the Civil War

(OK—the War Between the States), the Spanish–American War, World War I, World War II, the Korean War (or, if you please, the Korean conflict or even the Korean police action, as President Truman called it), the War in Vietnam, and the wars in Iraq. Why? Each would require a book in itself.

I am not trained or educated as a historian. (That will be more obvious to some readers than to others.) But I have been reading the newspaper every day for over fifty years and I have a warped, retentive mind. (When I was writing one of my baseball books, I remembered the incident at the 1967 World Series: Former Ambassador Joseph Kennedy had a fainting spell or an attack of some kind at Fenway Park during the game. His sons, U.S. Senators Robert and Teddy, attentively helped their father into his car, *then returned to the game.* That stayed with me, but the score and the opponent did not. I had to look them up.)

I have noted throughout the book odd and offbeat events because that's what interests me. World War II? Yes, that was important. But you can read about it in 2,625 other books. But what about the first patent for a yo-yo? The largest mass hanging in American history? The trials of Axis Sally, Tokyo Rose, and the only trial in U.S. Supreme Court history— where else are you going to find *those*?

I think the most interesting fact I learned while researching and writing this book is that the first foreign king to visit the United States (David Kalakaua of Hawaii) had been *elected* king. (See page 68.)

Please do not read this book if you are looking for a complete, definitive history of the United States.[1] There may be such a book, but it has become obsolete since you started reading this sentence. This book is not comprehensive. But it is fun. I hope you enjoy it.

Douglas B. Lyons

---

[1] The best single-volume history of the United States, and the funniest, is *Dave Barry Slept Here: A Sort of History of the United States.*

The Creation of a Nation

0–1799

"Freedom is never given; it is won."

A. Philip Randolph

THE LAND BRIDGE FROM SIBERIA

13,000 years ago. The land bridge across the Bering Strait permits people to walk (or at times to travel by boat) from Siberia to Alaska.

VIRGINIA DARE

August 18, 1587. Virginia Dare is born on Roanoke Island, Virginia, the first child born to European parents in the new world. Her mother is Eleanor White, and her father Ananias Dare.

JAMESTOWN

May 14, 1607. The first permanent European settlement in North America is established in Jamestown, Virginia.

THE MAYFLOWER COMPACT

November 21, 1620. As their ship lies at anchor off what is now Provincetown, Massachusetts, forty-one of the passengers on the *Mayflower* sign the Mayflower Compact, agreeing to be governed by it when they landed at Plymouth on December 21. This is the first recorded vote in the New World.

THE BRONX IS UP AND THE BATTERY'S DOWN

September 10, 1629. Jonas Bronk buys 500 acres from local Indians. The land is north of Manhattan, and is later named for him—the Bronx.

ROGER WILLIAMS, FOUNDER OF RHODE ISLAND, AND CHAMPION OF RELIGIOUS FREEDOM

1635. Roger Williams, ordained as a minister in the Church of England, arrives in Boston, Massachusetts, from England. He believes in religious freedom and seeks a split from the Church of England. His unpopular ideas include buying, rather than taking, land from Native Americans. By 1635, his religious views are considered so radical by the Puritans that he is tried and convicted. On October 9, 1635, he is banished from the colony.

In January, 1636, he purchases Native American land and forms the settlement of Providence, Rhode Island. The Providence Compact is signed on November 20, 1637. Among the tenets he establishes are separation of church and state, toleration, and democracy (one vote for each head of family). Rhode Island becomes a refuge for all those suffering from religious persecution.

The statue atop the Rhode Island Statehouse in Providence is not of Roger Williams, as many believe. A statue of Williams stands nearby in Roger Williams Park. The figure atop the statehouse is known simply as "Independent Man."

I'LL DRINK TO THAT!

1632. The first brewery in the New World is established in New Amsterdam by Peter Minuit. Pe-ter! Pe-ter! Pe-ter! Pe-ter! Pe-ter!

THIS IS HOW NEW YORK GOT A BAD REPUTATION

May 15, 1638. There is a fight between Jan Gybersten and Gerrit Jansen. Jansen is stabbed and dies—New York City's first recorded murder.

300 YEARS BEFORE PHIL FOSTER, BROOKLYN'S AMBASSADOR TO THE UNITED STATES

NOVEMBER 26, 1646. BREUCKELEN IS DECLARED A MUNICIPALITY BY THE DUTCH WEST INDIA COMPANY—THE FIRST IN NEW YORK STATE.

THE SALEM WITCH TRIALS

June–September, 1692. Nineteen convicted witches are hanged on Gallows Hill, near Salem, Massachusetts. Another refuses a trial, and is pressed to death by heavy stones.

THE BIRTH OF FREEDOM OF THE PRESS

August 5, 1735. The birth of freedom of the press in the United States—before there was a United States. In the town of Eastchester (now Mt. Vernon), New York, John Peter Zenger, a German-born immigrant, is one of two printers in the colony. On November 5, 1733, Zenger publishes the first issue of the *Weekly Journal.* In it, and in subsequent editions, he champions a free press and criticizes Royal Governor William Cosby. Finally, Cosby has had enough. The chief justice—a Cosby crony—asks a grand jury to indict Zenger for seditious libel. The grand jury refuses. The chief justice tries again, but, claiming that they could not tell who wrote the offending text, the grand jury again refuses to indict Zenger. Cosby offers a fifty pound reward for the names of the authors of the libels.

Cosby also directs his attorney general to file an information (an accusatory document) in court. Based on the information, the court issues an arrest warrant for Zenger.

Zenger is arrested on November 17, 1734. Bail is set at £800 and Zenger stays in jail for the next eight months.

The *Weekly Journal* only misses publishing for one week. Meanwhile, Zenger's trial starts on July 29, 1735 with the selection of a jury. Zenger concedes that he printed and published the libelous material. The question, says his lawyer Andrew Hamilton, is whether Zenger could publish "[t]he just complaints of a number of men who suffer under a bad administration." In short, was truth a defense in a libel action in the colonies? It was not under English law. And one of the two judges in Zenger's trial rules that it is not a defense in New York either. But the decision is still up to the jury.

But in charging the jury, the chief judge tells them that there is really nothing for them to decide. Zenger admits the publication. Therefore, there can be only one verdict—guilty. It will be up to the pro-government judges to decide, thereafter, what to do about the publication.

But the jury announces its verdict of not guilty, and the case is over. It was safe to criticize the government without fear of imprisonment.

MEET ME IN ST. LOUIS

February 15, 1764. Pierre Laclede Liguest and Rene August Chouteau found the city of St. Louis, Missouri. They agree, almost immediately, that the city cannot support two major league baseball teams.

THE BOSTON TEA PARTY

December 16, 1773. As a protest against the taxing of tea, "The Sons of Liberty," dressed as Mohawks, board three British ships in Boston's harbor—the *Beaver*, the *Eleanor*, and the *Dartmouth*. They dump 45 tons of tea overboard in what has become known as the "Boston Tea Party." Their cry of "no taxation without representation" reverberates to this day.

ANCHOR AWEIGH!

1775. What is a navy without a ship? The U.S. Navy gets its first ship—the schooner *Hannah*.

THE MIDNIGHT RIDE OF PAUL REVERE

April 18, 1775. A silversmith from Boston named Paul Revere rides through Lexington, Massachusetts, to warn John Adams, John Hancock, and other patriots that the British Army is going to be rowed across the Charles River. His ride is immortalized in 1860 in a poem by Henry Wadsworth Longfellow, "The Midnight Ride of Paul Revere."

THE SHOT HEARD AROUND THE WORLD

April 19, 1775. Shooting breaks out and the Revolutionary War starts at Lexington and Concord, Massachusetts.

THE FOUR-DAY RIDE OF ISRAEL BISSEL

April 19–24, 1775. Israel Bissel rides 345 miles in four days and six hours from Watertown, Massachusetts, through New Haven, New York City, and on to Philadelphia to deliver the message to colonists, "To arms, to arms, the war has begun!" Eighty-five years later, Henry Wadsworth Longfellow decided not to write of the four-day ride of Israel Bissel. Paul Revere had a nicer ring to it.

PATRICK HENRY, PATRIOT

April 23, 1775. At St. John's Episcopal Church, in Richmond, Virginia, in the presence of George Washington and Thomas Jefferson, Patrick Henry delivers a patriotic speech, ending with: "Gentlemen may cry, Peace, Peace—but there is no peace. The war is actually begun! The next gale that sweeps from the north will bring to our ears the clash of resounding arms! Our brethren are already in the field! Why stand we here idle? What is it that gentlemen wish? What would they have? Is life so dear, or peace so sweet, as to be purchased at the price of chains and slavery? Forbid it, Almighty God! I know not what course others may take; but as for me, give me liberty or give me death!"

THE DEATH OF NATHAN HALE

September 22, 1776. In New York City, Nathan Hale is hanged by the British as a spy. His last words: "My only regret is that I have only one life to give for my country."

A NEW NATION IS BORN

July 4, 1776. Philadelphia, Pennsylvania. The Declaration of Independence, written by Thomas Jefferson—one of the most important documents in history—is signed by 56 patriots from 13 states.

FORMING A NATION—1777–1799

December 20, 1776–February 27, 1777. The Second Continental Congress, trying to avoid the British, leaves Philadelphia. It meets at Henry Fite's house in Baltimore. Now, Baltimore is the nation's capital.

March 4–September 18, 1777. The Second Continental Congress returns to Philadelphia, which is, once again, the capital of the United States.

Other capitals where the Continental Congress meets include the old Courthouse in Lancaster, Pennsylvania (September 27, 1777); New York City (September 30, 1777–June 27, 1778); the French Arms Tavern—then the largest building in the city—in Trenton, New Jersey (November 1, 1784–December 24, 1784); back to New York City (January 11, 1785–Fall, 1788; March 4, 1789–August 12, 1790); and finally, on July 16, 1790, Washington, District of Columbia, is created as the permanent capital of the United States. It is sixty-nine square miles.

THE MIDNIGHT RIDE OF SYBIL LUDINGTON

April 26, 1777. Sixteen-year-old New Yorker Sybil Ludington rides forty miles at night to rouse the countryside to the impending attack by the British.

THE ARTICLES OF CONFEDERATION

November 15, 1777. The Articles of Confederation are agreed to by the second Continental Congress and are in effect from March 1, 1781. This is the first formal document uniting the original thirteen colonies. The Articles of Confederation govern the nation until June 21, 1788, when the Constitution is finally ratified. During this time, John Hanson, Elias Boudinot, Thomas Mifflin, Richard Henry Lee, John Hancock, Nathan Gorman, Arthur St. Clair, and Cyrus Griffin serve one-year terms as president of the United States.

THE BRITISH SURRENDER

October 19, 1781. After six years of bitter war, the British have had enough. In a ceremony at Yorktown, Virginia, the British army surrenders. The band aptly plays "The World Turned Upside Down."

THE BATTLE AFTER THE WAR

August 19, 1782. Blue Licks, near Mount Olivet, Kentucky, is the site of the last battle of the American Revolution. The battle of Blue Licks occurred ten months after Cornwallis surrendered at Yorktown.

THE REVOLUTIONARY WAR IS OVER

September 3, 1783. The Treaty of Paris is signed, formally ending the Revolutionary War.

FAREWELL TO THE TROOPS

December 4, 1783. General Washington bids farewell to his troops at New York City's Fraunces Tavern.

FEDERALIST #1

November 20, 1787. *Federalist No. 1* is published. *The Federalist Papers*, probably written by Alexander Hamilton, James Madison, and John Jay, appears in a newspaper in New York. The eighty-five essays argue persuasively in favor of a federal constitution.

THE FIRST STATE

December 7, 1787. Delaware becomes the first state to ratify the new Constitution. That's why Delaware's license plates proclaim it to be "The First State." Connecticut's license plate used to proclaim Connecticut the "Constitution State." It was the first state with a written constitution.

THE CONSTITUTION IS RATIFIED

June 21, 1788. New Hampshire approves the Constitution of the United States—the ninth state to do so. This action ratifies the Constitution, and it is effective from this date.

WASHINGTON ELECTED

April 30, 1789. After being elected president of the United States by a unanimous electoral vote, General George Washington is sworn in in New York City—the first elected head of state. During his inauguration he quotes Genesis 49:13, a page chosen at random and in haste. Washington serves two terms: April 30, 1789–March 3, 1797.

THE SIX-MEMBER SUPREME COURT OF THE UNITED STATES

The Supreme Court of the United States, created by Section I, Article III of the Constitution of the United States, is established with six members in 1789. The Court's first session is held on February 2, 1790.

THE BILL OF RIGHTS

DECEMBER 15, 1791. THE FIRST TEN AMENDMENTS TO THE CONSTITUTION OF THE UNITED STATES—THE BILL OF RIGHTS—ARE RATIFIED.

THE CORNERSTONE OF THE CAPITOL

September 18, 1793. The cornerstone of the Capitol is laid in Washington, D.C., by George Washington in a Masonic ceremony.

THE XITH AMENDMENT

February 11, 1795. The XIth Amendment to the Constitution of the United States is ratified.

JOHN ADAMS ELECTED

November 3, 1796. John Adams is elected president and serves March 4, 1797–March 3, 1801. He is the first president to live in the White House, when Washington, District of Columbia, becomes the young nation's capital.

HAIL AND FAREWELL, GEORGE WASHINGTON

December 14, 1799. George Washington, first president of the United States, dies at his beloved home, Mt. Vernon, Virginia.

Growing Pains

1800–1849

"The will of the people is the only legitimate foundation of any government, and to protect its free expression should be our first object."

Thomas Jefferson

JEFFERSON–BURR, JEFFERSON–BURR. STOP. YOU'RE BOTH RIGHT. IT'S A TIE!

1800. The presidential election of 1800 ends in a tie between Aaron Burr and Thomas Jefferson, each with seventy-three electoral votes. Actually, Jefferson is running for president, and Burr for vice president on the same ticket, against John Adams and Charles Pinckney, but the electoral voters do not specify whether their votes for Burr are for president or vice president.

The election is decided by the House of Representatives, where each state has one vote. With sixteen states at the time, nine votes are needed for an outright victory. The voting lasts from February 11–February 17, 1801, with no winner. On February 17, on the *twenty-sixth ballot*, Jefferson prevails with ten votes and becomes president. Burr is vice president.

1801. The membership of the Supreme Court of the United States is reduced from six members to five in 1801, increased from five to seven in 1807, from seven to nine in 1837, and from nine to ten in 1863. (Didn't anybody think that having an appellate court with an even number of judges might not be such a good idea???) In 1866, it was decreased from ten to seven. The final change was in 1869 when the number was increased from seven to nine, where it remains.

MARBURY V. MADISON

February 24, 1803. The Supreme Court, led by Chief Justice John Marshall (the first to be called "Chief Justice of the United States," rather than "of the Supreme Court"), decides *Marbury v. Madison*, establishing the principles of judicial review and of judicial supremacy—the right of the Supreme Court to declare a legislative act unconstitutional.

THE LOUISIANA PURCHASE

April 30, 1803. President Thomas Jefferson pays $15,000,000 to Napoleon of France to buy not only the city of New Orleans, but the entire Louisiana Territory—at 800,000 square miles, over twenty-two percent of the modern United States. With the stroke of his quill, he adds territory that will become Arkansas, Montana, Nebraska, North Dakota, Oklahoma, South Dakota, and Wyoming. The Senate ratifies the treaty on December 20, 1803, and the deed is done. The United States doubles in size for three cents per acre.

But the land needs to be explored. Jefferson designates his personal secretary, Meriwether Lewis, and Captain William Clark to lead the thirty-three-member "Corps of Discovery" to explore the new territory and report back to Jefferson.

On May 14, 1804, the Lewis and Clark expedition embarks on its journey. They are to explore the Missouri River and its tributaries, the Columbia River, the Colorado, and the Oregon territory to the Pacific in an effort to open up the new land for trade. Before leaving, Lewis and Clark study zoology, ornithology, medicine, and cartography, among other scientific disciplines. Their journals, complete with hundreds of sketches of Native Americans they met, plants and trees they had never seen before, and animals they encountered, including prairie dogs and grizzly bears, are an incredibly detailed account of their two-year journey.

They return to St. Louis, Missouri, on September 23, 1806.

THE XIITH AMENDMENT TO THE CONSTITUTION

June 15, 1804. The XIIth Amendment to the Constitution is ratified. It provides for separate election for the president and vice president via the Electoral College—so that there is no repeat of the election of 1800. Previously, the top vote-getter became president and the runner-up vice president—even if they had different policies and came from different parties.

TAKE TEN STEPS. TURN. FIRE.

July 11, 1804. The site: Weehawken, New Jersey. The duelists: Aaron Burr, the vice president of the United States, and Alexander Hamilton, America's first secretary of the treasury. They fight over a supposed slur uttered by Hamilton about Burr. Burr shoots and kills Hamilton.

DON'T I KNOW YOU FROM SOMEWHERE?

August 17, 1805. In one of the most incredible and serendipitous events in American history, Meriwether Lewis and William Clark's expedition to the west, to explore the new Louisiana Purchase[1], needs horses. As they near what they later name "Camp Fortunate" (near what is now the Clark Canyon Reservoir in Dillon, Montana), they are approached by a band of Shoshone Native Americans. Lewis and Clark do not know whether the Shoshone wish them well or ill. The Shoshone do not know Lewis and Clark's intentions, either. But the explorers' interpreter and guide, Sacagawea, a young Shoshone woman, traveling with Lewis and Clark along with her husband Toussaint Charbonneau and baby Jean Baptiste, recognizes one of the Shoshone band *as her brother Cameahwait*! There is much joy in both groups, as the siblings have not seen each other for years. The expedition is saved.

On January 1, 1807, Lewis returns to the White House for the first time in four years, and meets President Jefferson.

---

1 Their two-year mission: to seek out and explore new worlds and new civilizations. To boldly go where no men have gone before. And that was, what, 4,000 years before Capt. James Tiberius Kirk of the Starship Enterprise?

GROWING PAINS

JAMES MADISON SERVES TWO TERMS AS PRESIDENT OF THE UNITED STATES
March 4, 1809. Five-foot-four, one-hundred-pound James Madison is president March 4, 1809–March 3, 1817. He became the last surviving signer of the Constitution.

THE WAR OF 1812
June 12, 1812. The United States declares war on Great Britain, primarily because of British impression of American soldiers, i.e., forcing them into the British military.

WASHINGTON TORCHED
August 24, 1814. The White House is burned, the Capitol torched, and the city of Washington is captured by the British during the War of 1812.

THE STAR-SPANGLED BANNER

September 14, 1814. Lawyer Francis Scott Key sees the enormous American flag (now on display at the Smithsonian) flying over Ft. McHenry, in Baltimore harbor, despite a twenty-five-hour British bombardment. He writes a poem, "The Star-Spangled Banner," which is set to the music of an old song, "To Anacreon in Heaven." The song does not officially become the national anthem until March 3, 1931, when it is so designated by President Herbert Hoover.

THE WAR OF 1812 ENDS

December 24, 1814. The Treaty of Ghent is signed, ending the War of 1812.

ONE LAST BATTLE IS FOUGHT, EVEN THOUGH THE WAR IS OVER

January 8, 1815. The Americans and the British fight the Battle of New Orleans—even though the War of 1812 has already been ended by the Treaty of Ghent. The American forces, led by General Andrew Jackson, with help from Jean Lafitte, the pirate, win their most decisive battle. Unfortunately, news that the war had ended did not reach them in time.

THE ORIGINAL FLORIDA LAND DEAL

February 22, 1819. Florida is purchased from Spain through the Adams–Onís Treaty of 1819. Through the negotiating efforts of U.S. Secretary of State John Quincy Adams, the United States purchases Florida from Spain for five million dollars.

UP, UP, AND AWAY

1820. Stephen Long explores the southwestern part of the Louisiana Purchase. His historian, Dr. Edwin James, makes the first recorded climb of Pike's Peak in Colorado. James Peak is named for him.

REMEMBER THE ALAMO

The Alamo was built in 1724 as the Mission San Antonio de Valero in what is now San Antonio, Texas. On February 23, 1826, Mexican General Santa Anna attacks the mission, which has become a fortress defended by Texans. For thirteen days, the Texans hold out. The defenders include frontiersmen Jim Bowie and Davy Crockett. But, even with two hundred reinforcements, they cannot hold out and on March 6 Santa Anna's army overwhelms the defenders and captures the Alamo, which has since become a symbol of Texas's independence.

THE PRESIDENTIAL ELECTION OF 1824 ENDS IN A TIE

February 9, 1825. Although Andrew Jackson wins a plurality of the popular and the electoral votes, he does not win by enough to claim the presidency. John Quincy Adams is still in the race. Henry Clay, the third-place finisher, throws his support to Adams, then drops out of the race. The House of Representatives votes thirteen to eleven (each state getting one vote) to make Adams the sixth president. Clay is named secretary of state in what many see as a sleazy deal. Jackson is livid, but bides his time. He beats Adams in 1828. Adams later serves in the House of Representatives, the only ex-president to do so. John Quincy Adams is the first president to be photographed.

TWO FOUNDING FATHERS DIE FIFTY YEARS AFTER THE DECLARATION OF INDEPENDENCE WAS SIGNED

July 4, 1826. In one of the great coincidences in American history, John Adams and Thomas Jefferson both die on the fiftieth anniversary of the Declaration of Independence. Adams's last words are "Thomas Jefferson survives."

Thomas Jefferson served as president of the United States from March 4, 1801 to March 3, 1809. Apparently, Jefferson didn't think much of his eight years in office. The obelisk marker on his grave at his home in Monticello, Virginia, notes that he is the father of the Declaration of American Independence, of the Statute of Virginia for Religious Freedom, and father of the University of Virginia. The marker says nothing about his four years as vice president (1797–1801, under John Adams) or eight years as president.

THE BOOK OF MORMON

1827. Joseph Smith claims to have had three visions, and further claims that he was visited in Palmyra, New York, by the previously unknown Angel "Maroni," who revealed to him the location of the Golden Plates on a hill in Manchester, in Ontario County, New York.

Accompanying the Plates are two stones, "Urim" and "Thummin," which are used to help translate the Book of Mormon, which Smith dictates from behind a curtain in 1830, based on the Plates.

Smith and his Mormon followers move to Kirtland, Ohio, then to Nauvoo, Illinois, where they are unwelcome. He runs for president, is "sealed" polygamously to over twenty women, and declares martial law in Nauvoo. Eventually, he flees across the Mississippi to Carthage, Illinois, where he surrenders. But on June 27, 1844, he is shot and killed by an angry mob while in jail.

Brigham Young, who, as President of the Quorum of Twelve Apostles, has been Smith's right-hand man, takes up the reigns of leadership of the Mormons. Young leads the Mormons west, eventually to the Salt Lake Valley in what is now the state of Utah, on July 24, 1847.

Utah first applies for statehood in 1849 as the state of "Deseret."

Young becomes governor of Utah territory, but in 1852 he declares that plural marriage is an integral part of Mormon Church law.

President James Buchanan sends troops to put down the Mormon rebellion against federal authority.

On May 10, 1869, the "Golden Spike" is hammered home, joining the Union Pacific and the Central Pacific— the first transcontinental railroad. The two lines meet at Promontory Point, Utah. With the railroad, settlers come to Utah, including many who are not Mormon.

Brigham Young dies on August 29, 1877.

The Mormon Church renounced polygamy in 1890 as the cost of becoming a state, which it did on January 4, 1896.[2]

[2] The history of Joseph Smith, Brigham Young, the Mormons, and the State of Utah are the subjects of many books, studies, and analyses. Because of the nature of this book, I have severely but I hope accurately condensed this complicated and fascinating history. Like all of the entries in this book, the text above is not the comprehensive, definitive, all-inclusive probing history, analysis, and appreciation of the founding of the Mormon Church and Utah's path to statehood that the subjects command. And it should not be seen as such.

GOLD! IN DAHLONGA, GEORGIA!

October 27, 1828. Gold is discovered in Dahlonga, Georgia. The first U.S. gold rush is on. In 1838, the U.S. mint starts making five-dollar gold coins in Dahlonga.

"AMERICA"

1831. Samuel Francis Smith writes the lyrics to "America" ["My Country, 'Tis of Thee"] in Andover, Massachusetts. It was first sung on July 4, 1831, at the Park Street Church in Boston, to the tune of "God Save the King (or Queen)."

OBERLIN IS INTEGRATED AND CO-ED

September 2, 1833. Oberlin College opens—the first co-ed college in the country, and the first to admit blacks.

THE LITTLE MAGICIAN

1836. Martin van Buren, also known as "Martin van Ruin" and the "Little Magician," is elected president of the United States and serves one term, from March 4, 1837 to March 3, 1841. He is the first president who was born a citizen of the United States.

THE PULASKI EXPLODES

June 14, 1838. The steamship *Pulaski* explodes off the coast of North Carolina. A hundred lives are lost. In the aftermath of the tragedy, Congress makes inspection of commercial ships a federal responsibility.

DING DONG

July 8, 1835. The Liberty Bell is said to have developed a crack while tolling the death of Chief Justice John Marshall two days before. Marshall served as chief justice longer than any man in history, before or since—thirty-four years, five months, and two days, from 1801 to 1835.

The Liberty Bell was purchased by Pennsylvania in 1751 to commemorate the fiftieth anniversary of the 1701 Pennsylvania Charter of Privileges. The Bell contains a quote from Leviticus, 25:10: "Proclaim Liberty throughout all the land unto all the inhabitants thereof."

TIPPICANOE AND TYLER TOO

March 4, 1841. William Henry Harrison—nicknamed Tippecanoe because, as a general, he had won the Native American campaign Battle of Tippecanoe in Indiana—is elected president of the United States. Born in 1773, he is the last president who was born before the Revolutionary War. He serves March 4, 1841–April 4, 1841, the shortest presidency in American history. Harrison is president-elect longer than he is president.

Harrison delivers the longest inaugural speech in history—an hour-and-forty-five-minute, 8,500-word speech in a snowstorm—catches pneumonia at his own inauguration, and dies a month later. He is the first president to die in office.

John Tyler ("Tippecanoe and Tyler, too!") becomes the first vice president to succeed to the presidency. Tyler, born in 1790, is the first president who was not a British subject. He is sworn in as the tenth president on April 6, 1841 by U.S. Circuit Court Judge William Cranch at Brown's Hotel in Washington, D.C. Tyler was known as "His Accidency."

Nine years later, on July 10, 1850, Cranch also swears in Millard Fillmore in the House chamber, upon the death of Zachary Taylor. Cranch thus becomes the only non-chief justice to swear in two presidents.

FIRST TELEGRAPHED NEWS

May 1, 1844. The first news to be sent by telegraph is that the Whigs had nominated Henry Clay for president. The message is sent from Annapolis Junction, Maryland, to the Capitol in Washington, D.C.

FIRST TELEGRAPHED MESSAGE

May 24, 1844. Annie Ellsworth (the daughter of one of Morse's friends) chooses a biblical passage from Numbers 23:23: "What hath God wrought*?" as the first message to be transmitted via Morse Code by Samuel F.B. Morse, from the Supreme Court's Chamber in the Capitol to Morse's partner Alfred Vail in Baltimore.

* Wrought, for those of you paying attention, is the past tense of wreak.

TEXAS JOINS

December 29, 1845. The Republic of Texas joins the Union as the 28th state. Texas retains the right to split itself into five separate states.

THE SMITHSONIAN

August 10, 1846. President James K. Polk signs into law an act to establish the Smithsonian Institution in Washington, D.C.

THE OLDEST PUBLIC LIBRARY

1848. The Boston Public Library opens. It's the oldest free lending library in the United States.

NIAGARA FALLS STOP FALLING

March 29–30, 1848. Because of an ice jam in the upper river, Niagara Falls stop falling. The Falls don't freeze, but the flow of water stops for a few hours and people walk out on the riverbed, searching for lost artifacts.

On August 14, 1849, Francois Gravelot, known as "Blondin," walked over Niagara Falls on a tightrope 1,100 feet long and three inches in diameter, carrying his manager Harry Colcord on his back.

THE TREATY ENDING THE MEXICAN WAR

February 2, 1848. The Treaty of Guadalupe-Hidalgo is signed by the United States and Mexico, ending the Mexican War. Mexico cedes 200,000 square miles to the United States, including what is now most of Arizona, California, Colorado, New Mexico, and Utah. Mexico also gives up its claims to Texas.

WOMEN'S RIGHTS

July 19–20, 1848. The first convention to promote women's rights is held at the Wesleyan Methodist Church in Seneca Falls, New York. Among those attending are Elizabeth Cady Stanton, Lucretia Mott, and Frederick Douglass.

I'VE NEVER VOTED FOR A LOSER

1849. Zachary Taylor is elected president. The first vote he ever cast was for himself in the presidential election.

Expansion and Division

1850–1899

"Government of the people, by the people, for the people, shall not perish from the Earth."

Abraham Lincoln, 1863

SINGS LIKE A BIRD

September 11, 1850. Jenny Lind, "The Swedish Nightingale," makes her American debut in New York City, presented by P.T. Barnum. Barnum promotes Lind's American tour so well that 40,000 (yes, forty thousand) are on hand to welcome Lind when her boat docks in New York.

MASSACHUSETTS ADOPTS THE FIRST ADOPTION LAW

1851. MASSACHUSETTS PASSES THE "ADOPTION OF CHILDREN ACT," THE FIRST MODERN ADOPTION LAW.

UNCLE TOM'S CABIN

June 5, 1851–April 1, 1852. Uncle Tom's Cabin, *by Harriet Beecher Stowe, is published, first in a magazine called* National Era. *When it is published in 1852 in book form, the antislavery novel sells 300,000 copies, an enormous figure for the day. When Stowe is introduced to President Lincoln in 1862, he is said to have remarked, "So you are the little woman who wrote the book that started this great war!"*

A GREAT DAY IN HISTORY—THE INVENTION OF
THE POTATO CHIP
1853. At a swank hotel in Saratoga Springs, New York,
chef George Crum invents the potato chip.

I DO SOLEMNLY AFFIRM...

March 4, 1853. Franklin Pierce—the first
president born in the nineteenth century—is the
only man to take the Presidential Oath of Office
by affirming, rather than swearing. Franklin
Pierce's signature is five inches long.

THE GADSDEN PURCHASE

December 30, 1853. The United States buys nearly 30,000
square miles from Mexico—what is now southern Arizona
and New Mexico—in the Gadsden Purchase. James Gadsden
was the U.S. Minister to Mexico. The price is a bargain:
45,535 square miles/30,000,000 acres for about thirty-
three cents an acre.

FOURTEEN PLEASE

MAY, 1854. AT THE CRYSTAL PALACE EXPOSITION IN NEW YORK CITY, ELISHA GRAVES OTIS DEMONSTRATES HIS NEW SAFETY ELEVATOR BRAKE. HE HAS HIMSELF RAISED ON AN ELEVATOR PLATFORM, THEN HAS THE CABLE CUT. THE SAFETY BRAKE, WHICH HE INVENTED, PREVENTS THE ELEVATOR FROM MOVING. THIS SAFETY DEVICE HELPS MAKE ELEVATORS POPULAR, AND TALL BUILDINGS SAFE.

TAKE THAT!

May 22, 1856. Using his gold-topped cane, U.S. Representative Preston Brooks of South Carolina beats antislavery Senator Charles Sumner of Massachusetts on the floor of the Senate. Sumner had delivered a speech called "The Crime Against Kansas," a state that was fast becoming known as "bleeding Kansas." As a result of the beating, Sumner is unable to return to the Senate for three years due to his injuries.

EXPANSION AND DIVISION

JOHN BROWN

May 24, 1856. Five proslavery settlers are killed in Pottawatomie, Kansas, on May 24, 1856, by a band of seven led by John Brown. On May 21, the antislavery town of Lawrence, Kansas, had been beset by white supremacists who looted and burned the town.

John Brown was an admirer of Nat Turner, who led an armed slave revolt in Virginia that killed fifty-five whites on August 13, 1831.

On October 16, 1859, Brown and his small band of zealots cut telegraph wires around Harper's Ferry, Virginia (soon to be West Virginia). His plan was to capture the federal arsenal at Harper's Ferry to arm and lead a slave revolt himself. Things do not go well for Brown, and he winds up holding more than thirty hostages in the armory. Nearby slaves do not immediately revolt. Shots are exchanged, and Oliver Brown, one of John Brown's sons, is killed. At 11 p.m., Robert E. Lee arrives, commanding a company of United States Marines. Brown refuses to surrender and the marines storm the armory. Brown and four of his men are captured.

Brown's trial for treason against Virginia, inciting slaves to rebellion, and murder starts on October 26, 1859, in Charles Town. Brown is convicted and, on December 2, is hanged. Guarding the hanging site are cadets from the Virginia Military Institute under the command of Thomas (later "Stonewall") Jackson and soldiers led by Robert E. Lee. Also present is a volunteer with the Virginia Greys—one John Wilkes Booth, Abraham Lincoln's assassin.

THE DRED SCOTT CASE

March 6, 1857. The Supreme Court of the United States issues one of its most notorious, reviled decisions: *Scott v. Sandford.*

Dred Scott was a slave. He sued his master in Missouri, demanding his freedom. Scott had lived as a free man in the slave-holding state of Missouri, and claimed the benefit of the "once free, always free" doctrine.

The Court rules, 7–2[1], in a decision by Chief Justice Roger B. Taney, that slaves are not "citizens," and that they have no rights of citizenship. The Court also holds that the federal government can not prohibit slavery in federal territories.

The Dred Scott case helps crystallize the national debate over slavery.

---

[1] Each justice writes a separate opinion—a rarity on the Supreme Court.

THE PONY EXPRESS

From April 3, 1860 (at 7:15 p.m., to be exact), through October 24, 1861, young riders weighing less than 125 pounds speed west at about ten miles per hour, carrying the U.S. Mail from St. Joseph Missouri nearly 2,000 miles through Kansas, Nebraska, Colorado, Wyoming, Utah, and Nevada to Sacramento, California. They change riders every seventy-five to one hundred miles, and change horses every ten to fifteen miles at about 150 change stations. Ten days is typical for a letter from Missouri to California, but their fastest run is said to be seven days and seventeen hours, when the riders carry copies of President Lincoln's first Inaugural Address.

With the completion of the first transcontinental telegraph system in 1861, messages can get across the continent in seconds, not days, and the Pony Express fades into history.

The legendary riders of the short-lived Pony Express helped shrink the nation.

LINCOLN ELECTED

November 6, 1860. Abraham Lincoln of Illinois, known as "Honest Abe" and "The Rail Splitter," is elected president of the United States. Lincoln is the first president whose inauguration, on March 4, 1861, is photographed.

THE SURRENDER OF FORT SUMTER

April 11, 1861. Brigadier-General P.G.T. Beauregard of the Provisional Forces of the Confederate States of America demands the surrender of Union troops at Fort Sumter, in Charleston, South Carolina. The beleaguered Union troops refuse. At 4:30 a.m. on April 12, a ten-inch mortar shell is fired at the fort—the first shot of the Civil War. Nobody is killed during the exchange of shots. On April 13, the Union soldiers surrender, and the fort is evacuated on April 14.

On April 15, President Lincoln issues a call for 75,000 volunteers to fight the rebels.

THEY CAN'T STOP IT

1861. At the start of the Civil War, five men who served as president of the United States are alive: Martin van Buren, John Tyler, Millard Fillmore, Franklin Pierce, and James Buchanan. They are unable to stop the rush toward war.

LINCOLN SUSPENDS HABEAS CORPUS

July 2, 1861. President Lincoln suspends the writ of habeas corpus *in some cases.*

TEN SENATORS EXPELLED

July 11, 1861. The United States Senate, by a vote of thirty-two to ten, expels ten of its own members—all Southern senators whose states had voted to secede from the Union. Other Southern senators simply leave, resign, or have their terms expire.

WE ARE A BAND OF BROTHERS

November 6, 1861. Jefferson Davis, U.S. senator from Mississippi, and the son-in-law of President Zachary Taylor, is elected to a six-year term as president of the Confederate States of America.

"THE BATTLE HYMN" OF THE REPUBLIC

February, 1862. The *Atlantic Monthly* publishes Julia Ward Howe's lyrics to "The Battle Hymn of the Republic."

THE *MONITOR* AND THE *MERRIMAC*

March 9, 1862. The first battle of ironclad warships is fought near Hampton Roads, Virginia. The U.S.S. *Monitor* and the C.S.S. *Virginia*, (formerly the Union ship *Merrimac*) fight to a four-and-a-half-hour draw. But the battle sounds the death knell for wooden war ships.

WE WILL ALL HANG TOGETHER

December 26, 1862. In the largest mass hanging in American history, thirty-eight Santee Sioux are hanged together in Mankato, Minnesota.

THE EMANCIPATION PROCLAMATION

January 1, 1863. President Lincoln signs and issues the Emancipation Proclamation, declaring that "all persons held as slaves" in the Confederate States "are, and henceforward shall be, free."

I JUST WANT A SMALL WEDDING

February 10, 1863. Charles Stratton and Lavinia Warren are married before 2,000 people in Grace Church in New York City. Stratton is one of the most famous people in America, although he is not a politician, an athlete, an inventor, a corporate magnate, or a military man—though he uses a military name. Stratton is, however, an entertainer of sorts— P.T. Barnum taught him how to sing and dance—better known as General Tom Thumb. He is thirty-three inches tall and weighs fifteen pounds, while twenty-year-old Lavinia Warren is thirty-two inches tall and weighs twenty-nine pounds.

After the wedding, the Strattons are received at the White House by President Lincoln.

GETTYSBURG

July 3, 1863. The decisive Union victory that halts the Confederate's northern advance is won in a small town in Pennsylvania—the Battle of Gettysburg.

THE FIRST THANKSGIVING HOLIDAY

August 6, 1863. Thanksgiving becomes an official holiday proclaimed by President Lincoln to be observed on the last Thursday in November.

THE GETTYSBURG ADDRESS

November 19, 1863. President Lincoln takes the train 65 miles from Washington to Gettysburg, Pennsylvania, for the dedication of a Union cemetery just four and a half months after one of the most decisive battles of the Civil War. This marked the Confederacy's last hurrah in the North.

Before Lincoln speaks, Edward Everett speaks for two hours.

Legend has it that Lincoln scribbled some notes in pencil on the back of an envelope. What emerged were ten sentences and approximately 280 words. The speech takes just a matter of minutes. But despite Lincoln's belief that "the world will little note, nor long remember what we say here," the Gettysburg Address will be remembered as long as the English language is spoken.

Four score and seven years ago our fathers brought forth on this continent, a new nation, conceived in Liberty, and dedicated to the proposition that all men are created equal.

Now we are engaged in a great civil war, testing whether that nation, or any nation so conceived and so dedicated, can long endure.

We are met on a great battle-field of that war.

We have come to dedicate a portion of that field, as a final resting place for those who here gave their lives that that nation might live.

It is altogether fitting and proper that we should do this.

But, in a larger sense, we can not dedicate—we can not consecrate—we can not hallow—this ground.

The brave men, living and dead, who struggled here, have consecrated it, far above our poor power to add or detract.

The world will little note, nor long remember what we say here, but it can never forget what they did here.

It is for us the living, rather, to be dedicated here to the unfinished work which they who fought here have thus far so nobly advanced.

It is rather for us to be here dedicated to the great task remaining before us—that from these honored dead we take increased devotion to that cause for which they gave the last full measure of devotion—that we here highly resolve that these dead shall not have died in vain—that this nation, under God, shall have a new birth of freedom—and that government of the people, by the people, for the people, shall not perish from the earth.

ARLINGTON DEDICATED

May 13, 1864. Arlington National Cemetery, overlooking the District of Columbia on 1,100 acres in Virginia, is the final resting place for 250,000 veterans as well as President and Chief Justice William Howard Taft, President John F. Kennedy, and the Tomb of the Unknowns.

William Christman of the 67th Pennsylvania Infantry is the first soldier to be buried there on May 13, 1864. Soldiers from every American war are interred at Arlington.

MARCHING THROUGH GEORGIA

September 2, 1864. Brigadier General William Tecumseh Sherman of the Union Army orders Atlanta evacuated. His soldiers burn anything of military value, and continue their march to the sea. On December 22, he takes Savannah, and presents it to President Lincoln and the Union as a Christmas gift.

SURRENDER

April 9, 1865. At the home of Wilmer McLean in the village of Appomattox Courthouse, Virginia, General Robert E. Lee surrenders the Army of Northern Virginia to Lieutenant General Ulysses S. Grant, commander of the Army of the Potomac. The Civil War, which had taken 620,000 lives, was over.

PRESIDENT LINCOLN ASSASSINATED

April 14, 1865. At Ford's Theater in Washington, D.C., while watching *Our American Cousin*, starring Laura Keene, Abraham Lincoln, the sixteenth president of the United States, is shot in the back of the head with a .50 caliber bullet by actor John Wilkes Booth. Booth jumps to the stage from the president's box, shouting "*Sic Semper Tyrannis!*" [Latin for "Thus always to tyrants" the Virginia state motto]. Lincoln is taken to Peterson House across the street from the theater, where he dies on April 15.

Booth escapes the theater, but is shot and killed by a soldier named Boston Corbett on April 26, 1865, in a barn in northern Virginia.

ANDREW JOHNSON IMPEACHED BUT ACQUITTED

Andrew Johnson of Tennessee becomes the country's seventeenth president upon the death of Abraham Lincoln. Johnson is the first president who is neither a lawyer nor a professional soldier. He is sworn in at Washington's Kirkwood Hotel by Chief Justice Salmon P. Chase on April 15, 1865.

On August 14, 1866, Johnson becomes the first president to be visited by a queen—Queen Emma of the Sandwich Islands (Hawaii).

Johnson antagonizes members of Congress by demanding that he be permitted to select his own cabinet officers, rather than retaining all of Lincoln's choices. Congress passes the Tenure of Office Act in 1867 over Johnson's veto. It requires the same Senate approval for *firing* a cabinet officer as has been required for *confirming* one. But Johnson balks, claiming that the law unconstitutionally ties the hands of the executive. On February 2, 1868, Johnson fires Secretary of War Edwin Stanton. But Stanton locks himself in his office, refusing to leave.

On February 24, 1868, the House of Representatives votes eleven articles of impeachment by a tally of 126 to 47. As prescribed by Article I, Section Three, Clause Six of the Constitution, Johnson is tried by the United States Senate on three articles, with Chief Justice Salmon Portland Chase (secretary of the treasury under Lincoln, whose face adorns the noncirculating $10,000 bill) presiding. A two-thirds vote is needed to convict him and remove him from office—an event unprecedented in America's history.

But the anti-Johnson faction garners only thirty-five of the thirty-six votes needed. Edmund G. Ross of Kansas casts the deciding vote to acquit Johnson on each count, and on May 16, 1868,

Johnson is acquitted by a vote of thirty-five to nineteen—one short of the two-thirds needed to convict.

In *Profiles in Courage* (which won the Pulitzer Prize in 1957), then-Senator John F. Kennedy wrote that by his vote in the impeachment trial of Andrew Johnson, Ross had done more to save the Union than any man in history.

Only one other president has been impeached by the House: Bill Clinton, by a House vote of 228 to 206 on December 20, 1998. He too was acquitted by the Senate.

THE SULTANA *EXPLODES*

April 26, 1865. One of the worst steamboat disasters in American history—the demise of the steamship Sultana. *Around 1,500 returning Civil War veterans take the sternwheeler* Sultana *for the voyage home. Among the passengers are many who had spent time at Andersonville, the Confederate prison for captured Union soldiers (see page 60). The ship weighs 1,719 tons and has a crew of eighty-five, including Captain J.C. Mason.*

On April 21, the Sultana *sails from New Orleans on her way up the Mississippi.*

The Sultana*'s boiler explodes at night when the ship is just a few miles from Memphis. Most of the passengers are sleeping. Many jump overboard, preferring to try to swim, rather than being burned alive. The water is near freezing.*

Because there is no ship's manifest, the exact number killed in the tragedy is hard to pinpoint, but it was somewhere between 1,500 and 1,900.

I JUST FOLLOWED ORDERS

November 10, 1865. Capt. Henry Wirz of the Confederate Army is hanged in Washington, D.C., after the first war crimes trial in American history. He is convicted of conspiracy and murder for acts committed as the commandant of the Confederate prison camp at Andersonville, Georgia, probably the worst place in American history. There, 45,000 captured Union soldiers are held in abominable conditions from February, 1864 to May, 1865. Twenty-nine percent die. Wirz, a native of Switzerland, claims throughout his two-month trial before a military panel of Union officers that, as a soldier in the Confederate Army, he was just following orders. The guilty verdict rejected that defense.

THE XIIITH AMENDMENT

December 6, 1865. The XIIIth Amendment to the Constitution of the United States, outlawing slavery, is ratified. Mississippi votes not to ratify this Amendment.

IT HAS ITS UPS AND DOWNS

November 20, 1866. The first U.S. patent for a yo-yo is issued to James L. Haven and Charles Hettrick. At least twenty-one yo-yo patents follow.

BRIDGE OVER THE OHIO RIVER

January 1, 1867. The John A. Roebling Suspension Bridge opens, spanning the Ohio River from Cincinnati, Ohio, to Covington, Kentucky. It is the longest suspension bridge in the world. With time out for the Civil War, the bridge took ten years to complete.

NEBRASKA, FUTURE HOME FO THE WORLD'S LARGEST PORCH SWING, JOINS THE UNION[2]

March 1, 1867. Nebraska joins the Union as the 37th state.

[2] Yes it's true. The world's largest porch swing is in Hebron, Nebraska. It holds 24 children or 18 adults.

NORTH TO THE FUTURE

October 18, 1867. After months of negotiations between Secretary of State William Seward and Edouard de Stoeckl, the Russian minister to the United States, the purchase of Alaska from Russia is complete, and the territory—all 586,412 square miles—is transferred to the U.S. in one of the most incredible real estate deals since the purchase of Manhattan Island for twenty-four dollars. The purchase price, $7,200,000, means that Alaska, which will become the forty-ninth state, was sold for approximately $127.63 per acre. Alaska is twice the size of Texas, and 425 times the size of Rhode Island.

THE XIVTH AMENDMENT

July 9, 1868. The XIVth Amendment to the Constitution of the United States is ratified. This Amendment makes the protections and prohibitions of the first ten Amendments—the Bill of Rights—applicable to the states.

LOCK IT UP

1868. LINUS YALE JR. INVENTS THE CYLINDER LOCK. IT'S STILL IN USE.

THE CARDIFF GIANT

October 16, 1869. One of the great hoaxes of American history is the "Cardiff Giant." A ten-foot tall stone man was "found" behind William Newell's barn in Cardiff, New York. People from neighboring towns come by the thousands to his farm to see it. Even when Newell started charging fifty cents a peek, they still come.

Is it a petrified man? Is it an ancient statue? Just how old is it? Was the biblical report (Genesis 6:4) that "There were giants in the earth in those days" true?

No. The Giant was the creation of George Hull. He had the Giant made for about $2,600 and Newell is in on the scheme. The Giant is such a great money-maker that it is sold for $37,500, and moved to a larger and more accessible exhibit in Syracuse.

When a paleontologist from Yale examines the Giant, finds chisel marks, and brands it a fake, Hull admits the fraud. But people still come to see "Old Hoaxey."

P.T. Barnum, the greatest showman and exhibitor of hokum of the day, offers $60,000 for the Giant—an enormous sum for the time. When the offer is rejected, Barnum simply builds his own copy—a copy of a fraud.

Today, the Cardiff Giant is on exhibit at the Farmer's Museum in Cooperstown, New York.

THE GOLDEN SPIKE

May 10, 1869. In Promontory, Utah, the "Golden Spike," joining the Union Pacific and the Central Pacific railroads, is driven. The connection of the two railways creates the nation's first transcontinental railroad.

HOW INVENTIVE!

1869–1910. Thomas Alva Edison averages one patent every eleven days. His total of 1,093 patents is still the record.

THE XVTH AMENDMENT

February 3, 1870. The XVth Amendment to the Constitution of the United States, extending the right to vote to African-Americans, is ratified. The Amendment is rejected by Tennessee.

A COMPLETELY DISPOSABLE PRODUCT

1871. A patent is issued to Seth Wheeler, an unsung hero of American inventiveness. The patent is for perforated, rolled, toilet paper.

THE GREAT CHICAGO FIRE

October 8, 1871, 9 p.m. A fire starts in a cow barn at 137 DeKoven Street in Chicago, owned by Patrick O'Leary.

By 1:30 a.m., Chicago's business district is in flames. The fire spreads to the rest of the city. When it is over, the "Great Chicago Fire" has killed 300 people, left 90,000 homeless, and caused property damage estimated at nearly a quarter billion dollars.

YELLOWSTONE NATIONAL PARK CREATED

March 1, 1872. With the stroke of his pen, President Ulysses S. Grant signs into law a bill making 2.2 million acres of Montana and Wyoming into Yellowstone, the first National Park. At 3,472 square miles, the park is bigger than Delaware and Rhode Island combined.

SENATOR ANDREW JOHNSON

November 2, 1874. Tennessee elects ex-president Andrew Johnson to the Senate. He serves from March 4, 1875, until his death on July 31, 1875. Johnson is buried with his head resting on a copy of the Constitution.

While Andrew Johnson is the only ex- or former president to serve in the Senate after his service as president, he is not the only former vice president to do so: after his term as vice president (1965–1969), Hubert Humphrey of Minnesota returns to the Senate, 1971–1978.

EARMUFFS

1873. The Greenwood Champion Ear Protector, better known as earmuffs, are invented in by Chester Greenwood of Farmingham, Maine. He patented the device in 1877.

ALOHA!

November 28, 1874. The first king to visit the United States is David Kalakaua (birth name: David La'amea Kamanakapu'u Mahinulani Nalaiaehuokalani Lumialani Kal'kaua) of the Kingdom of Hawaii. His ship docks in San Francisco. David Kalakaua had been *elected* king by the Royal Hawaiian legislature. (How many other *elected* kings can *you* name?) President Grant holds a dinner for the king. Before Kalakaua eats anything, three tasters try it. Grant (1822–1885) lived during the lifetime of thirty presidents. By the way, if you're starting a collection of short books, try "The speeches of President Grant." He gave none.

IT'S FOR YOU

March 10, 1876. "Mr. Watson, come here. I want to see you." With these words, spoken by inventor Alexander Graham Bell, a revolution in communications is started—the invention of the telephone.

CUSTER

June 25, 1876. Lieutenant-Colonel George Armstrong Custer leads 210 soldiers of the Seventh Cavalry to their doom at the hands of Lakota, Cheyenne, and Arapaho at the Little Bighorn in what is now Montana.

THE PLOT TO STEAL ABRAHAM LINCOLN'S BODY

November 7, 1876. On election day, a gang of would-be grave robbers starts executing an audacious plan to rob (actually, burglarize) the grave of Abraham Lincoln, sixteenth president of the United States, in Oak Ridge Cemetery in Springfield, Illinois. Their plan is to demand a ransom of $200,000. The gang, lead by "Big Jim" Kinealy has been infiltrated by a U.S. Secret Service Agent named Lewis G. Swegles. Once the thieves have pried the marble lid of the crypt, they instruct Swegles to bring the wagon around so they can steal Lincoln's wooden casket, which they have partially removed. Swegles leaves, but returns with eight detectives, hiding nearby. But the thieves escape. They are arrested ten days later in Chicago. Eight months later, they go to trial. Although they are convicted, the maximum sentence is only one year in prison. Stealing a buried body is not yet a crime in Illinois.

AAA+88

August 2, 1876. While playing poker, and looking at what becomes known as the "Dead Man's Hand"—aces and eights—James Butler "Wild Bill" Hickock is shot and killed in Deadwood City, Dakota Territory. The killer is Jack McCall. McCall is later tried, convicted, and hanged.

PRESIDENT TILDEN OR PRESIDENT HAYES

November 7, 1876. Samuel J. Tilden has more popular votes than his opponent, Rutherford B. Hayes. With 185 electoral votes needed for victory, Tilden has 184 and Hayes has 165. The electoral votes of Florida, Louisiana, South Carolina, and Oregon are in dispute. Congress establishes an Electoral Commission to investigate and select a winner. Hayes is selected, and on March 3, 1877, Rutherford Birchard Hayes is sworn in as the nineteenth president of the United States in a secret ceremony at the White House. President Hayes has neither an inaugural parade nor a ball.

PLAY IT AGAIN, PLEASE

While it is difficult to fix a date on which something was invented, August 12, 1877 is generally recognized as the date on which Thomas Alva Edison completed his work on the phonograph. Now, the human voice— whether speaking or singing, as well as music and other sounds—can be recorded, mass produced, and replayed.

YELLOW FEVER

1878. An outbreak of yellow fever—fever, chills, pains, hemorrhaging, black vomit, and jaundiced skin—strikes Memphis, Tennessee. (Yellow fever is said to have been so named for the "yellow jack," or yellow flag of quarantine, flown over infected ships.) In 1873, a yellow fever epidemic had taken 2,000 lives in Memphis, but this is worse. Much worse. The first death is reported on August 13, 1878. About 25,000 people leave the city in two weeks to escape the disease, but 17,000 are infected and 5,150 die. Ninety percent of the white population of Memphis contracts the disease, and seventy percent of them die. For unknown reasons, only seven percent of the city's black population dies.

It is not until 1900 that Major Walter Reed of the United States Army, conducting experiments in Cuba, discovers a link between yellow fever and *Aedes aegypti* mosquitoes. Reed had already discovered the source of typhoid fever, then common at all military bases.

Reed and the twenty-four soldiers (many of whom volunteer to be infected) who conduct the experiments that lead to the discovery of the source of yellow fever receive special Congressional gold medals for their heroic work. (Some medals are given to their survivors.) Reed died in 1902. His monument at Arlington says: "He gave to man control over that dreadful scourge, yellow fever."

THE GREAT GRASSHOPPER PLAGUE

1878. Minnesota's wheat farmers have been devastated by five summers of infestation of Rocky Mountain Locusts. Nearly seventy percent of the farmed land in the state is farmed for wheat. The farmers diversify to introduce other crops.

QWERTY

1878. The QWERTY pattern for the modern typewriter (and later word processor and computer) keyboard is patented by Christopher Sholes. The keyboard arrangement is the most common in use today for English. The longest word which can be created on one line of a QWERTY keyboard is TYPEWRITER.

THIS TIME, IT REALLY IS FOR YOU

1879. President Rutherford B. Hayes has the first telephone and the first bathtub installed in the White House. He gets phone number "1." Hayes is also the first president to have a typewriter in the White House.

THE RED CROSS
May 21, 1881. Clarissa "Clara" Barton founds the American Red Cross.

PRESIDENT JAMES A. GARFIELD ASSASSINATED

July 2, 1881. James A. Garfield, the twentieth president of the United States—and the first who is left-handed—is shot in the arm and back by Charles Guiteau at the Baltimore and Potomac Railway station in Washington, D.C. Garfield dies on September 19. Guiteau is arrested and tried. His trial lasts from November 14, 1881, to May 22, 1882. Guiteau is convicted and hanged in the District of Columbia jail on June 30, 1882.

PRESIDENT CHESTER ALAN ARTHUR

September 20, 1881. Upon the death of President Garfield, Vice President Chester Alan Arthur is sworn in as the nation's twenty-first president by Justice John R. Brady of the New York State Supreme Court at Arthur's New York City home at 123 Lexington Avenue. Two days later, he repeats the oath in the vice president's office in the Capitol in Washington, D.C., where the oath is administered by Morrison R. Waite, Chief Justice of the United States.

GUNFIGHT AT THE O.K. CORRAL

October 26, 1881. One of the most famous events in the history of the old West—the gunfight at the O.K. Corral, in Tombstone, Arizona Territory. Brothers Wyatt, Virgil, and Morgan Earp, and John Henry "Doc" Holliday (a dentist), representing the law, shoot Ike and Bill Clanton, and Tom and Frank McLaury. Holliday, Morgan Earp, and Virgil Earp are wounded. Ike Clanton, who was unarmed, survives. Billy Claiborne, who ran through the fight, also survives. Thirty shots were fired in thirty seconds.

ON, OFF, ON, OFF

September 4, 1882. The first commercial electric power station becomes operational. It provides electrical power and lights within a one-square mile area in lower Manhattan.

THE BROOKLYN BRIDGE

May 23, 1883. The Brooklyn Bridge, connecting the City of Brooklyn and the island of Manhattan, is dedicated by President Chester Arthur and New York Governor Grover Cleveland.

CRAYONS

1885. Joseph Binney, his son Edward Binney, and C. Harold Smith, a nephew, form a partnership in 1885. They manufacture pigment for barn paint and carbon black for car tires. Later, they produce pencils and chalk for schools.

In 1903, Binney and Smith introduce a box of eight Crayola crayons (black, green, brown, blue, red, violet, orange, and yellow), which sells for five cents. The word "Crayola" is suggested by Alice Binney, Edward's wife. It comes from the French: "craie" for chalk and "ola" for "oleaginous."

THE PRESIDENT WEDS

June 2, 1886. Forty-nine-year-old President Grover Cleveland, serving the first of his two non-sequential terms (which means he is both the twenty-second and the twenty-fourth president), weds twenty-one-year-old Frances Folsom in the Blue Room—the only president to marry in the White House. Their first daughter Ruth has a candy bar named for her—Baby Ruth. The Clevelands' second daughter Esther is born on the second floor in the White House on September 9, 1893—the only presidential baby ever born in the White House.

THE LADY OF THE HARBOR

October 28, 1886. The Statue of Liberty, created by Auguste Bartholdi, a gift from the people of France, comes to America as 350 individual pieces in 214 crates. It is reassembled in four months on Bedloes Island in New York Harbor. The poem on its pedestal, by Emma Lazarus, is "The New Colossus":

> Not like the brazen giant of Greek fame,
> With conquering limbs astride from land to land;
> Here at our sea-washed sunset gates shall stand
> A mighty woman with a torch, whose flame
> Is the imprisoned lightning, and her name
> Mother of Exiles. From her beacon-hand
> Glows world-wide welcome; her mild eyes command
> The air-bridged harbor that twin cities frame.
> "Keep ancient lands, your storied pomp!" cries she
> With silent lips. "Give me your tired, your poor,
> Your huddled masses yearning to breathe free,
> The wretched refuse of your teeming shore.
> Send these, the homeless, tempest-tost to me,
> I lift my lamp beside the golden door."

BRRR

March 11–14, 1888. The Blizzard of '88. One of the worst blizzards in history, certainly the worst in 100 years, hits New York City and the East Coast from Maryland to Maine. More than 400 people perish. Damage is estimated at $25 million.

Fifty inches of snow falls in Connecticut and Massachusetts, and forty in New York. Snowdrifts are up to fifty feet high.

CASEY AT THE BAT

JUNE 3, 1888. THE SAN FRANCISCO *EXAMINER* PUBLISHES A POEM BY ERNEST LAWRENCE THAYER: "CASEY AT THE BAT." IT BECOMES THE MOST FAMOUS OF BASEBALL POEMS.

THIS MADE PAULY SHORE AND ERNEST POSSIBLE
October 17, 1888. Thomas Alva Edison patents a "kinetoscope," a device for making motion pictures. Movies are born.

FIRST ELECTROCUTION

August 6, 1890. Convicted ax-murderer Walter Kemmler of Buffalo is the first person put to death by the state of New York in Auburn Prison using a new method: the electric chair. Electrocution as a means of legal execution becomes popular in many states.

WOUNDED KNEE

December 29, 1890. Shooting breaks out during peace talks at Wounded Knee, South Dakota, between Sioux chief Big Foot and U.S. Army officers. Some 300 Sioux are killed, including Big Foot, as well as twenty-five soldiers. The massacre at Wounded Knee marks the last battle in the Indian Wars.

LUCKY THEY WERE NOT MADE IN TRUTH OR CONSEQUENCES, NEW MEXICO, OR KING OF PRUSSIA, PENNSYLVANIA

1891. Fig-filled cookies are named for the city where they are first manufactured—Newton, Massachusetts.

P.T. BARNUM'S PREMATURE OBITUARY

April 8, 1891. Phineas Taylor Barnum lay dying at "Marina," his home in Bridgeport, Connecticut. He asked the newspapers, for whom he had done so much ("The Feejee Mermaid," George Washington's 171-year-old nurse, Col. Tom Thumb, Jenny Lind, the "Egress"), to do him a favor: Could they please print his obituary before he died, so he could read it? They did.

ELLIS ISLAND

January 1, 1892. Ellis Island, in the upper bay of New York Harbor, opens. It is the first spot where European refugees enter the United States. Between that date and November 29, 1954, when it closes, approximately 12 million people pass through Ellis Island. The peak year is 1907, when 1.25 million immigrants are admitted through Ellis Island. Today, it is a museum. More than 100 million Americans have an ancestor who came through Ellis Island.

THE OKLAHOMA LAND RUSH

September 16, 1893. At precisely 12 noon, a cannon booms on a piece of land known as the Cherokee Strip, and 100,000 settlers are off—the Oklahoma Land Rush is on, the biggest land rush in Oklahoma Territory's history. There are only 42,000 plots, so the race is between the "Boomers," who wait for the cannon's boom, and the "Sooners," who literally jump the gun. Natives of Oklahoma are still called "Sooners."

COXEY'S ARMY

March 25, 1894. Jacob S. Coxey leads a group of marchers from Ohio to Washington, D.C. Their intent is to try to persuade Congress to create public works programs to provide jobs to many who are unemployed. "Coxey's Army" picks up supporters on its way, and by the time they reach the capital, on April 30, they are 500 strong—the first protest march in the capital. But Coxey is arrested for walking on the Capitol grass, and the marchers disperse.

THE PULLMAN STRIKE

May 11, 1894. Pullman Palace Car Company workers strike in Chicago. The president of the American Railway Union is Eugene Victor Debs. Soon, 50,000 workers are on strike and there is no railroad traffic in or out of Chicago. A federal judge issues an injunction to stop the strike, and federal troops are sent to enforce it. The strike is broken and Debs is jailed for disobeying the injunction.

ROTATE!

1895. THE FIRST GAME OF VOLLEYBALL (INVENTED BY WILLIAM G. MORGAN) IS PLAYED IN HOLYOKE, MASSACHUSETTS.

"AMERICA THE BEAUTIFUL"

July 4, 1895. The lyrics to "America the Beautiful," by Katharine Lee Bates, are published, for the first time, in the *Congregationalist*. She says the lyrics came to her after a visit to Pike's Peak in Colorado. Bates revises the lyrics in 1904 and again in 1913.

SEPARATE BUT EQUAL

May 18, 1896. The United States Supreme Court issues its notorious decision in *Plessy v. Ferguson*. The Court finds, seven to one, that "separate but equal" facilities for blacks and whites are constitutional.

Justice John Marshall Harlan is the lone dissenter, writing: "There is no caste here. Our Constitution is color-blind, and neither knows nor tolerates classes among citizens."

Plessy was overruled by *Brown v. Board of Education* fifty-eight years later.

THE STARS AND STRIPES FOREVER

December 25, 1896. John Philip Sousa, "The March King," is on a ferry in Europe. A march comes to him complete. Upon his return, he writes it down just once, exactly as it came to him: "The Stars and Stripes Forever."

GOLD!

1898. Gold! The Nome Gold Rush is on: The gold of Nome is actually on the beach—forty miles of it. During the summer of 1899, over two million dollars in gold is found.

REMEMBER THE *MAINE!*

February 15, 1898. The U.S.S. *Maine* sinks after a still unexplained explosion in Havana, Cuba. The mast of the *Maine* is now part of the *Maine* Memorial at Arlington National Cemetery.

The sinking of the ship and the rallying cry "Remember the *Maine!*" help propel the United States into a war with Spain, which is declared on April 25, 1898.

THE GREAT AMERICAN PAPER CLIP

November 9, 1899. William D. Middlebrook patents the paper clip.

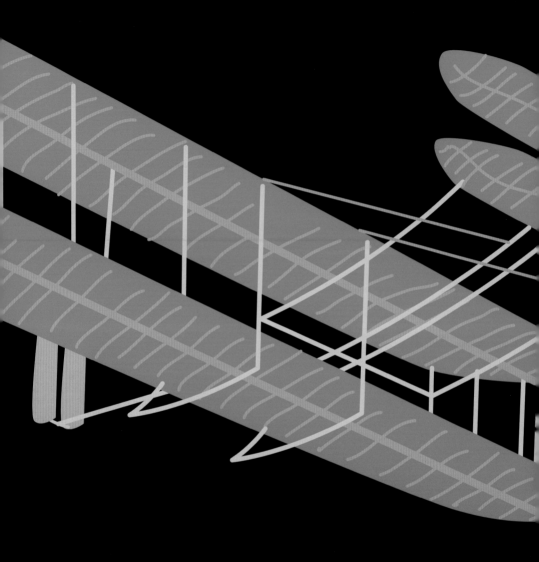

Tension and Turmoil

1900–1949

"You know, doing what is right is easy. The problem is knowing what is right."

Lyndon B. Johnson

A DEVASTATING HURRICANE WITH NO NAME

September 8, 1900. A devastating hurricane hits the coastal city of Galveston, Texas. Over 8,000 people are killed and much of the city destroyed in just a few hours. Nearly 3,000 homes are swept away.

PRESIDENT WILLIAM MCKINLEY ASSASSINATED

September 6, 1901. William McKinley, the twenty-fifth president of the United States and the first one whose inauguration was captured on moving pictures, is shot by Leon Czolgosz at the Pan-American Exposition in Buffalo. McKinley dies eight days later on September 14. Czolgosz is arrested, tried, and convicted. He dies in the electric chair on October 29, 1901 at New York's Auburn Prison, just forty-five days after the shooting.

Vice President Theodore Roosevelt is located while hiking in the Adirondacks and, after a trip by wagon and train, on September 14 at Wilcox Mansion, 641 Delaware Avenue in Buffalo, New York, he is sworn in as president of the United States at 3:31 p.m. by U.S. District Court Judge John R. Hazel. As a boy of seven, Roosevelt had watched the funeral procession for Abraham Lincoln.

Roosevelt—the first president to ride in a car—helps popularize the name "White House" for the president's official residence.

YUM

1900. THE MILK CHOCOLATE HERSHEY BAR IS INTRODUCED.

WHY DO THEY CALL THEM NECCO WAFERS?

1901. The New England Confectionery Company introduces a new candy, named for its acronym: NECCO Wafers.

LINCOLN EXHUMED

September 26, 1901. The body of Abraham Lincoln, sixteenth President of the United States, is exhumed in Oak Ridge Cemetery in Springfield, Illinois, and examined. Thirty-six years after his death on April 15, 1865, his features are still recognizable. The body is reburied in a newly built crypt, where, it was thought, it could not be stolen.

WELCOME TO THE WHITE HOUSE

October 16, 1901. President Theodore Roosevelt invites Booker T. Washington, founder of the Tuskegee Institute in Alabama, to the White House—one of the first times a black man enters the White House through the front door.

OHIO'S UNIQUE FLAG

May 9, 1902. Ohio adopts its state flag, known as the *Ohio Burgee*, designed by John Eisemann. Ohio's is the only swallowtail state flag.

FIRST NATIONAL WILDLIFE REFUGE

March 14, 1903. President Theodore Roosevelt signs a measure creating Pelican Island in Florida as the first National Wildlife Refuge. By 2007, there are over 500 national wildlife refuges, covering nearly 95 million acres.

FIRST GAME OF THE FIRST WORLD SERIES

October 1, 1903. The first game of the first modern World Series is played at the Huntington Avenue Grounds in Boston between the Pittsburgh Pirates and the Boston Americans (Red Sox). Pittsburgh wins the game seven–three, but Boston wins the best-of-nine series five–three.

A TORCH TO LIGHT THE WAY

August 26, 1903. Conrad Hubert patents the cylindrical flashlight.

FIRST POWERED FLIGHT

December 17, 1903. Brothers Orville and Wilbur Wright, bicycle shop owners from Dayton, Ohio, achieve sustained powered flight for the first time, something people have dreamed about since they first looked up. At Kill Devil Hills on the North Carolina coast near Kitty Hawk, with Wilbur Wright at the controls, their biplane Flyer achieves powered flight for twelve seconds—a flight of 852 feet. Those twelve seconds change the world.

Since 1981, North Carolina license plates have proclaimed it "First in flight," with a rendering of the Wright brothers' plane. Ohio's plates name it the "Birthplace of aviation."

HELEN KELLER

1904. HELEN KELLER IS GRADUATED CUM LAUDE WITH A BACHELOR OF ARTS DEGREE FROM RADCLIFF COLLEGE. SHE CAN NEITHER SPEAK, SEE, NOR HEAR. HER TEACHER ANNE SULLIVAN HELPS HER COMMUNICATE.

HANG THAT UP

January 25, 1904. The wire hanger is patented.

THE *GENERAL SLOCUM* TRAGEDY

June 15, 1904. The steamboat *General Slocum* bursts into flame near 90 Street in New York's East River. The cause of the fire was thought to be a carelessly lighted match tossed into a barrel of straw. The crew has no training in putting out fires. Even worse, the ship's fire hoses are rotted, and burst when filled with water. The ship's captain, William van Schaick, decides not to dock the ship, fearing that he might ignite oil tankers already docked. So he presses on at full speed—fanning the flames—to North Brother Island, a mile away. The ship is equipped with 3,000 life jackets, but they too are rotted, and are no longer buoyant. 1,021 people—mostly children—die. Van Schaik is convicted of manslaughter and criminal negligence and sentenced to ten years at hard labor, later commuted to three years.

THE 1904 OLYMPICS IN ST. LOUIS

July 1, 1904. The third Olympics open in St. Louis, Missouri, as part of the Louisiana Purchase Exposition. The games are a sideshow, spread out over four months, as part of the World's Fair. These are the first games in which gold, silver, and bronze medals are awarded for first, second, and third place. George Eyser, an American gymnast with a wooden leg, wins six medals.

NEW YORK CITY'S FIRST SUBWAY

October 27, 1904. New York City's first subway system opens, and 150,000 people ride for five cents.

THE ONLY TRIAL IN THE SUPREME COURT'S HISTORY

On February 9, 1906, Ed Johnson, a black man is convicted of raping a white woman in Chattanooga, Tennessee. On March 18, the Supreme Court of the United States issues a stay of execution, so it may consider whether the Sixth Amendment's guarantee of a fair trial is applicable to the states[1]. But the very next day, a mob enters the jail, grabs Johnson, and lynches him.

The Court is furious that its order had been ignored.

A U.S. Department of Justice investigation finds the local prosecutor and judge complicit in the lynching. At a meeting of Chief Justice Melville Fuller, Associate Justice John Marshall Harlan, and U.S. Attorney General William Moody—later a Justice of the Supreme Court—it is decided that those responsible will be charged with criminal contempt of the Supreme Court—a charge never before brought.

The Supreme Court itself will conduct the trial—the first and still the only one in its history.

Twenty-seven residents of Chattanooga, including Sheriff Joseph Shipp and eight deputies, are charged by the Department of Justice with conspiracy to lynch Johnson. On December 24, 1906, the Court rules unanimously that it has jurisdiction to try the case.

The first part of the trial opens in Chattanooga on February 12, 1907. A special master is appointed to hear the witnesses in

Tennessee and report to the full Court. Charges against seventeen conspirators are dismissed and in March 1909 the trial moves to Washington, where the Supreme Court hears closing arguments.

Charles Bonaparte, Attorney General of the United States, argues for the government—an indication of how seriously the government views it.

The Court announces its decision on May 24, 1909. In a six–three, decision the Court finds Shipp and five others guilty. The rest are acquitted. Those convicted are brought before the Court on November 15, 1909 for sentencing. Chief Justice Fuller sentences them to between sixty and ninety days in jail.

After serving his sentence in the District of Columbia jail, Shipp returns to Tennessee, where he is greeted by a jubilant crowd of 10,000, singing "Dixie."

On February 24, 2000, Ed Johnson's ninety-four-year-old conviction for rape is overturned.

[1] The answer was not a foregone conclusion. Many believed that the Constitutional protections of the first ten amendments applied only to the *federal* government, and that the states were not bound by them. Over the years, though, in many cases, the Court has made the Bill of Rights applicable to the states through the 14th Amendment.

THE BIG ONE

April 18, 1906. An earthquake virtually destroys San Francisco, California, in one of the worst natural disasters in the nation's history. Nearly 500 city blocks and 25,000 buildings are reduced to rubble in one minute. Seven hundred die as a result of the quake and the three-day fire that follows.

THE PURE FOOD AND DRUG ACT

June 30, 1906. Embarrassed by muckraking books such as Upton Sinclair's *The Jungle*, Congress passes the Pure Food and Drug Act and the Meat Inspection Act.

THE FIRST NATIONAL MONUMENT

September 24, 1906. President Theodore Roosevelt signs documents proclaiming the first National Monument: Devil's Tower in Wyoming.

SMACK!

July 1, 1907. The Hershey Candy Company introduces one of its most popular delicacies: The Hershey Kiss, complete with silver foil wrap.

THE GRAND CANYON REALLY IS GRAND

January 11, 1908. The Grand Canyon, all 1,218,376 acres of it, is designated a National Monument. It is declared a National Park on February 26, 1919. The Arizona canyon includes 25 species of fish, 300 different birds, 50 reptiles and amphibians, and 75 other species of animals.

THE OVAL OFFICE

October, 1909. President William Howard Taft has the White House remodeled, and is the first to use the Oval Office.

THE FOUNDING OF THE N.A.A.C.P.

February 12, 1909. The National Association for the Advancement of Colored People—the N.A.A.C.P.—is founded by W.E.B. DuBois.

THE TRIANGLE FIRE

March 25, 1911. There's a fire at the Triangle Shirtwaist Company in New York City—"The Triangle Fire"—in which 146 people are killed. Most are women working under sweatshop conditions with the doors locked. This tragedy leads to some workplace labor reforms.

THE FIRST INDIANAPOLIS 500, AT 74.6 MPH

May 30, 1911. The first 500-mile race is held at the Brickyard—the Indianapolis Motor Speedway. The cars drive over 3,200,000 bricks. The first winner is Ray Harroun, driving a car known as the "Marmon Wasp." His winning speed is 74.6 miles per hour.

FOUR CORNERS

February 14, 1912. The only place in America where four states meet is the Four Corners. It's in Utah, New Mexico, Colorado, and Arizona. It didn't become "official" until February 14, 1912, when the last of the four, Arizona, became a state. Four Corners is on Navajo Nation land, and is overseen by the Navajo Nation Parks and Recreation Department.

S.O.S.—THE *TITANIC* SINKS

April 15, 1912. After being struck by an iceberg, H.M.S *Titanic* of the White Star Line, said to be "unsinkable," sinks 350 miles off the coast of Newfoundland on her first voyage. While 868 survivors are rescued, 1,522 are lost as the largest passenger ship afloat goes down in a few hours. *Titanic* carried 20 lifeboats, about enough for one-third of the 2,200 passengers and crew.

T.R. SHOT

October 14, 1912. Milwaukee, Wisconsin. Theodore Roosevelt, former president of the United States, and the nominee of the Progressive "Bull Moose" Party for president, is shot just before making a campaign speech.

At the Gilpatrick Hotel, T.R. is shot at close range by saloon keeper John Schrank. But the bullet is stopped by Roosevelt's eyeglass case and a copy of the speech he is about to deliver. Shrank proclaims that "any man looking for a third term ought to be shot."

Roosevelt, an advocate of the vigorous life, goes ahead and delivers the nearly hour-long speech, reading from his bloody and lifesaving notes. Only after he concludes does he allow himself to be taken to a hospital. He has suffered only a flesh wound. Roosevelt continues to campaign for a return to the White House, but he and Republican candidate William Howard Taft lose to Democrat Woodrow Wilson.

Shrank is found insane and committed to an asylum.

VOTE FOR DEBS!

November 5, 1912. Eugene Victor Debs, the Socialist candidate, receives nearly 900,000 votes for president—six percent of the popular vote.

I'M GAGA FOR GOO GOO

1913. The Goo Goo Cluster (peanuts, caramel, marshmallow, and milk chocolate) is introduced. It's a hit!

PAY YOUR TAXES

February 3, 1913. The XVIth Amendment to the Constitution of the United States, authorizing an income tax, is ratified, despite being defeated in Connecticut, Rhode Island, and Utah.

POPULAR VOTE FOR SENATORS

April 8, 1913. The XVIIth Amendment to the Constitution of the United States, authorizing the direct election of United States senators, is ratified. Previously, state legislatures selected senators.

SEE THE U.S.A.

October 31, 1913. The Lincoln Highway, the first transcontinental American highway designed for cars, is dedicated. The highway runs through twelve states from New York to San Francisco.

WHAT IS 17 ACROSS?

December 21, 1913. For the first time, the New York *World* publishes a new form of entertainment—a crossword puzzle.

THE *LUSITANIA* SINKS

R.M.S. *Lusitania*, launched in 1906, is the first steamship with four propellers, and is the first ship weighing over 30,000 tons. She is also the first (and probably the last) British ship with four smokestacks.

On May 7, 1915, the *Lusitania* is struck without warning by two torpedoes fired by the German submarine U-20 off the coast of Ireland, and sinks in eighteen minutes. While 761 passengers and crew are rescued, 1,198 are not.

The sinking of the *Lusitania* on her way to New York City, with the loss of 128 American lives, helps propel the United States to enter the Great War on the side of Great Britain.

THE GREAT BOSTON MOLASSES FLOOD

January 15, 1919. Boston, Massachusetts. A cast-iron tank containing molasses, 50 feet above the street, breaks at 12:40 p.m., and 2.5 million gallons of the gooey, sticky stuff pours onto Commercial Street. The wall of molasses is at least 15 feet high, travels at 35 miles per hour, and destroys everything in its path. The molasses deluge kills 21, injures over 150, and destroys numerous buildings.

JOE HILL

November 19, 1915. Joe Hill, born Joel Hägglund in Gävle, Sweden, is killed by a firing squad in Utah. Hill, a labor organizer for the Industrial Workers of the World (I.W.W., the Wobblies) had been convicted of murder on flimsy evidence. Just before he dies, he instructs his supporters: "Don't mourn—organize!" Hill is more famous after his death than he had been in life, especially because of the labor organizing song "Joe Hill," written in 1936 by Alfred Hayes and Earl Robinson.

BRANDEIS APPOINTED

January 28, 1916. President Woodrow Wilson[2] appoints Louis Brandeis, one of the most famous lawyers in the country, and a founder of the American Zionist movement, to be an associated justice of the Supreme Court. Brandeis is the first Jew appointed to the Court. Brandeis is confirmed by a Senate vote of forty-seven to twenty-two and serves from June 5, 1916 until February 13, 1939. Brandeis becomes the champion of the right to privacy.

[2] Actually, Thomas Woodrow Wilson, Ph.D. His doctorate was in philosophy.

THE FIRST BIRTH CONTROL CLINIC

OCTOBER 16, 1916. MARGARET SANGER OPENS THE FIRST BIRTH CONTROL CLINIC IN NEW YORK CITY. SHE IS PROMPTLY ARRESTED.

FIRST WOMAN IN CONGRESS

November 7, 1916. Jeannette Rankin, Republican of Montana, is the first woman elected to Congress. She votes against U.S. entry into World War I and, in 1941, into World War II as well.

GREETINGS!

On May 18, 1917, the Selective Service Act is adopted, authorizing a military draft.

Although American men are still required to register with the Selective Service System when they turn eighteen, the military draft ended and the all-volunteer military was born on July 1, 1973.

DOUGHBOYS LAND IN FRANCE

July, 1917. After U.S. soldiers land in France to help repel "the Hun"(Germany), American Commander General John J. "Black Jack" Pershing's aide Col. C. E. Stanton speaks at the tomb of the Marquis de Lafayette, who had aided the Americans during the Revolutionary War. Said Stanton: "Lafayette, we are here!"

EUGENE VICTOR DEBS RUNS FOR PRESIDENT FROM PRISON

Eugene Debs runs for president with a unique campaign slogan: "Prisoner 9653 for President."

On June 16, 1918, Debs speaks in Canton, Ohio, to criticize the Espionage Act. He is arrested, tried, and convicted of interfering with the draft. Debs is sentenced to ten years in prison. But he runs for president anyway in 1920. From prison. Debs gets an astounding 919,799 votes. President Harding pardons Debs in December 1921.

SAN SIMEON

1919. Work begins on San Simeon. The private home of newspaper mogul William Randolph Hearst, the mansion, on 40,000 acres near San Luis Obispo, California, is the most ornate, palatial private home ever built in America. All-told, the 115-room main house, appropriately named "Casa Grande," and outlying guest houses comprise 56 bedrooms, 41 fireplaces, 61 bathrooms—41 in Casa Grande alone—and a 345,000-gallon outdoor swimming pool, perhaps the most beautiful ever built. It was given to the state of California in 1951, after Hearst's death, and is now a museum—"Hearst Castle."

PROHIBITION

January 16, 1919. The XVIIIth Amendment to the Constitution of the United States, ratified on January 16, 1919 (to take effect one year later), prohibits the manufacture, transport, and sale of alcoholic beverages. Prohibition, though perhaps well-intentioned, turns out to be one of America's worst experiments in legislating morality. It is a complete and abject failure almost from the start and breeds disregard, disrespect, and contempt for the law and for law enforcement officers who were sworn to uphold it.

Prohibition leads to the growth of organized crime in the United States, as rum runners and speakeasies abound throughout the country.

Politicians who support Prohibition (like Herbert Hoover, the Secretary of Commerce who was the successful Republican candidate for president in 1928) are "dry," while those who oppose Prohibition (like Democratic candidate Al Smith) are "wet."

The XXIst Amendment to the Constitution of the United States (ratified December 5, 1933) is universally known by just one word: "Repeal." The manufacture, transportation, and sale of liquor, although strictly regulated by the states, is legal again.

PRESIDENT WILSON SUFFERS A STROKE

October 13, 1919. President Woodrow Wilson suffers a debilitating stroke. He is incapacitated for seventeen months, virtually shut off not only from the American people, but from his cabinet, legislators, and his senior advisors.

His second wife Edith cares for him, speaks for him, and is considered by many the acting president. Wilson never fully recovers.

GERMANY SURRENDERS

November 11, 1919, 5 a.m. The scene: a railroad car at a siding in the forest of Compiègne, France. The event: Germany signs the armistice ending World War I. The fighting will end at 11 a.m.—the eleventh hour of the eleventh day of the eleventh month.

Inscribed later on a stone tablet in French: *HERE ON THE ELEVENTH OF NOVEMBER 1918 SUCCUMBED THE CRIMINAL PRIDE OF THE GERMAN REICH. VANQUISHED BY THE FREE PEOPLES WHICH IT TRIED TO ENSLAVE.*

The toll: over fifteen million dead, over twenty-two million wounded, and eight million missing or prisoners.

Twenty-one years later, the same railroad car is used on June 22, 1940 at 6:50 p.m. when the French surrender to the Germans, after France falls in twenty-seven days. That surrender ceremony takes fifteen minutes. The Germans have the site destroyed three days later, and the railroad car is taken to Berlin, where it is later destroyed.

SENATE DEFEATS U.S. ENTRY INTO THE LEAGUE OF NATIONS

January 19, 1920. Woodrow Wilson's dream to guarantee future world peace through American participation in the League of Nations is defeated by seven votes in the United States Senate, thirty-eight to fifty-three.

THE XIXTH AMENDMENT

August 18, 1920. The XIXth Amendment to the Constitution of the United States, granting women the right to vote, is ratified.

TEAPOT DOME

In 1921, President Warren G. Harding signs an executive order transferring oil reserves at Teapot Dome, Wyoming, from the Navy to the Interior Department. The following year, Secretary of the Interior Albert B. Fall authorizes the leasing of the oil fields to one Harry F. Sinclair, and the leasing of the Elk Hills, California, oil fields to Edward L. Doheny. The leases were authorized without competitive bidding. Doheny has lent Fall $100,000 interest-free. When Fall retires, Sinclair lends him a large amount of money. Fall is convicted of accepting bribes, fined $100,000, and sent to federal prison for a year. Doheny and Sinclair are acquitted on bribery charges, but Sinclair goes to prison for contempt of the Senate. He had hired private investigators to snoop on the jury.

WILLIAM HOWARD TAFT—PRESIDENT AND CHIEF JUSTICE

June 30, 1921. Warren G. Harding, the twenty-ninth President of the United States, nominates William Howard Taft, the twenty-seventh president, to be chief justice of the United States. Taft is confirmed by the Senate on the same day. Taft served as chief justice until just before his death in 1930.

Taft is the only man to hold the top jobs in two of the three branches of government. His widow, Helen, is the first president's wife to be buried at Arlington, next to him.

FIRST BROADCAST OF A BASEBALL GAME

August 5, 1921. The Phillies–Pirates game in Pittsburgh is the first to be broadcast on the radio. Harold Arlin is at the mike.

THE BLACK SOX: YOU ARE OUT

August 21, 1921. Despite a jury verdict acquitting them, newly installed Baseball Commissioner Kenesaw Mountain Landis bans eight Chicago White Sox players—the "Black Sox[3]"—from professional baseball. This is the worst scandal in the history of the "national pastime." Landis concluded that they either helped throw the 1919 World Series to the Cincinnati Reds, or knew about the plot. The eight never play professional baseball again. They are: "Shoeless" Joe

Jackson, Chick Gandil, Swede Risberg, Buck Weaver, Happy Felsch, Eddie Cicotte, Lefty Williams, and Fred McMullin.

[3] Many believe that the sobriquet "Black Sox" came into use a few years earlier. Because parsimonious team owner Charles Comiskey tried to charge his White Sox players for laundering their uniforms, many players protested by continuing to wear the uniforms unwashed—hence, "The Black Sox."

LIVING, BREATHING DINOSAURS

Conan Doyle accepts an invitation to attend the annual meeting of the Society of American Magicians, of which Harry Houdini is the president. At the end of the meeting, during which magicians perform their best tricks, Conan Doyle is introduced and, with virtually no introduction or explanation, shows a brief film of living dinosaurs—apparently, the first ever seen.

The New York *Times* is mystified. The next day, the *Times* runs a front-page article, with the headlines: DINOSAURS CAVORT IN FILM FOR DOYLE...SPIRITIST MYSTIFIES WORLD-FAMED MAGICIANS WITH PICTURES OF PREHISTORIC BEASTS.

Conan Doyle had had his fun. He later reveals that the "living dinosaurs" were part of a film based on his novel, "The Lost World." The director had lent him some footage from the film to mystify the magicians. The pioneering special effects are by Willis H. O'Brien, who later created "Mighty Joe Young."

THE UNKNOWN SOLDIER

October 23, 1921. In Chaions-sur-Marne, France, the bodies of American soldiers from cemeteries in Asine-Marne, Meuse-Argonne, Somme, and St. Mihiel have been collected. They are checked to ensure that nothing was known about their names, dates of birth or death, rank, or organization. These are indeed unknown soldiers who died during the Great War. What papers did exist about these four bodies are burned, another step to assure anonymity.

The next day, the four caskets are displayed identically in a mortuary room. Sergeant Edward Younger is chosen to select one. He circles the coffins three times, places white roses on the third casket from the left, and salutes.

The casket is taken to Paris and then to Le Havre, where, draped with an American flag, it is ceremoniously placed aboard the American cruiser *Olympia* for the trip to Washington, D.C.

The casket is interred at the Tomb of the Unknowns at Arlington National Cemetery on November 11. The inscription: "Here Rests In Honored Glory An American Soldier Known But To God."

Since then, an unknown soldier from every American war has been interred in the Tomb of the Unknowns.

PRESIDENT HARDING DIES

August 2, 1923. Senator Warren Gamaliel Harding, Republican of Ohio, is elected the twenty-ninth president of the United States—partially, it is said, because he *looks* like a president. Harding is the first president to ride to his inauguration in a car, and the first to speak publicly on the radio. But his administration is considered one of the most corrupt in the nation's history. (See page 105.)

Harding dies of a stroke on August 2, 1923 at the Palace Hotel in San Francisco after the first presidential visit to Alaska. He is the first president survived by his father, George Tyrone Harding.

SON, DO YOU SOLEMNLY SWEAR…?

August 3, 1923. Upon the death of President Harding, Vice President Calvin Coolidge is located at his home in tiny Plymouth Notch, Vermont, where a notary public is quickly found to administer the presidential oath of office. The ceremony is held by oil lamp on the morning of August 4, at 2:47 a.m. The notary is Coolidge's father, John Calvin Coolidge, making Calvin Coolidge the only president sworn in by his father. Coolidge is elected in his own right in 1924. His inauguration on March 4, 1925 is the first to be broadcast on the radio. He declines to run again in 1928.

February 12, 1924. "Rhapsody in Blue" has its first performance in a concert at New York's Aeolian Hall, with George Gershwin at the piano. Gershwin becomes a star.

LEOPOLD AND LOEB

May 21, 1924. Nathan Leopold Jr. and Richard Loeb kidnap and kill fourteen-year-old Bobby Franks in Chicago. Loeb, eighteen, is a student at the University of Chicago. Leopold, nineteen, is a well-known bird watcher. Loeb's father Albert is a millionaire in charge of Sears, Roebuck's mail-order business. Nathan Leopold Sr. is a wealthy executive.

While disposing of Frank's body, Leopold drops his unusual eyeglasses. The killers had planned an elaborate kidnap scheme, but that failed when their demands for $10,000 ransom, which they don't need, are not met. But the police surmise that the ransom note was written by a well-educated person, and ultimately match the type on the ransom note to Leopold's typewriter.

Both were admirers of German philosopher Friedrich Nietzsche and believed that, as "supermen," the laws that applied to others did not apply to them, because of their superior intellect. The crime is labeled a "thrill killing." It is also one of the first "crimes of the century." Leopold and Loeb tag along with reporters who are trying to find more details of the case.

The game warden at Wolf Lake, where Franks's body is found, identifies a frequent visitor as Nathan Leopold. Leopold is a neighbor of Franks. The police trace the glasses. Only three such pairs had been sold in Chicago. One was bought by Nathan Leopold.

Both boys confess to the crime but each blames the other for the actual killing of Bobby Franks. Their parents are desperate to save their sons from the hangman's noose, and they roust sixty-seven-year old Clarence Darrow from bed: would he take their sons' case? Darrow agrees, but not because of the million dollar fee—a fortune at the time. Darrow will use the case to argue against capital punishment.

The trial of Leopold and Loeb—one of a dozen or so cases dubbed "the trial of the century"—starts on July 21, 1924. Darrow does not ask for a change of venue, or a severance. Darrow offers to plead both defendants guilty. Darrow wants just one man—in this case Judge John R. Caverly, not a jury of twelve—to decide whether Leopold and Loeb would live or die. Darrow presents "alienists" (psychiatrists) who have examined the pair. The doctors testify to the boys' psychopathic personalities.

The state asks for the death penalty. In fact, the state *demands* the death penalty for the unprovoked, premeditated murder of a fourteen-year-old boy. Darrow begs and pleads for a sentence other than death. He explains why he waived a jury and pleaded his clients guilty:

"I know perfectly well that where responsibility is divided by twelve, it is easy to say: "Away with him."

But, your honor, if these boys hang, you must do it. There can be no division of responsibility here. You can never explain that the rest overpowered you. It must be by your deliberate, cool, premeditated act, without a chance to shift responsibility.

I know your Honor stands between the future and the past. I know the future is with me, and what I stand for here; not merely for the lives of these two unfortunate lads, but for all boys and all girls; for all of the young, and as far as possible, for all of the old. I am pleading for life, understanding, charity, kindness, and the infinite mercy that considers all. I am pleading that we overcome cruelty with kindness and hatred with love. I know the future is on my side. Your Honor stands between the past and the future. You may hang these boys; you may hang them by the neck until they are dead. But in doing it you will turn your face toward the past. In doing it you are making it harder for every other boy who in ignorance and darkness must grope his way through the mazes which only childhood knows. In doing it you will make it harder for unborn children. You may save them and make it easier for every child that some time may stand where these boys stand. You will make it easier for every human being with an aspiration and a vision and a hope and a fate. I am pleading for the future;

I am pleading for a time when hatred and cruelty will not control the hearts of men. When we can learn by reason and judgment and understanding and faith that all life is worth saving, and that mercy is the highest attribute of man."

Judge Caverly is persuaded and sentences Leopold and Loeb to life imprisonment for the murder, plus ninety-nine years' imprisonment for the kidnapping.

Loeb dies in Joliet state prison on January 28, 1936, slashed fifty-eight times with a straight razor by another inmate. Leopold is paroled in 1958 after thirty-three years in prison. He moves to Puerto Rico, where he works as an X-ray technician. Leopold dies in 1971.

J. EDGAR HOOVER

May 24, 1924. Twenty-four-year-old John Edgar Hoover becomes director of what would become the Federal Bureau of Investigation. He stays in the job for forty-eight years until his death on May 2, 1972.

MUSH, BALTO

Winter, 1925. In Nome, Alaska, a diptheria epidemic breaks out among native peoples who have no natural immunity to it. The governor decides that trying to fly serum into Nome is too dangerous because of blizzard conditions. Also, the only two planes in Alaska at the time have open cockpits. So, a relay of twenty dogsledders and one hundred dogs is used to deliver the 300,000 units of antitoxin from Nenana to Nome. The route takes them 674 miles in temperatures reaching −53° Farenheit. The final leg is driven by Gunnar Kaasen, whose lead dog is a Husky named Balto. The antitoxin arrives in time on February 2, 1925 and is handed to the only doctor in town. Many lives are saved. A statue of Balto is erected in New York City's Central Park. Balto makes a guest appearance at Madison Square Garden before an adoring crowd of 20,000. The Iditarod Trail Sled Dog Race, annual since 1973, commemorates the event. Upon his death on March 14, 1933 at the age of eleven, Balto is stuffed and displayed at the Cleveland Museum of Natural History, where he is still an exhibit.

THE MONKEY TRIAL

May 5, 1925. John T. Scopes, a twenty-four-year-old public-school science teacher in rural Dayton, Tennessee[4], is arrested for the crime of teaching Charles Darwin's Theory of Evolution. He is brought to trial—the "Monkey Trial." The Scopes case was and is one of the most famous (or infamous) trials—and one of the most important—in American history.

The trial is seen as a fight between the story of Creation, as written in the Book of Genesis, versus science. It quickly becomes the Bible versus Charles Darwin. Which side are you on?

The local prosecutor accepts the offer of "The Boy Orator of the Platte"—William Jennings Bryan, the nation's best-known Fundamentalist Christian—to prosecute for the State of Tennessee, although it had been thirty years since Bryan had practiced law. Bryan had been secretary of state under Woodrow Wilson and had been the Democratic nominee for president in 1896, 1900, and 1908. He was the best known Populist and speaker in the country. Bryan was known as "The Great Commoner." His "Cross of Gold" speech to the Democratic convention on July 9, 1896, in Chicago, is one of the most famous in American history.

The lead attorney for the defense is Clarence Darrow of Chicago, the nation's most famous lawyer and outspoken agnostic. He is a well-known champion of unpopular people and causes.

The trial starts on July 10, 1925. Because of the oppressive heat and the great public interest in the biggest thing ever to happen in Dayton—1,000 people come to the tiny courthouse, with 300 standing—Judge John T. Raulston conducts some court sessions outdoors.

The government quickly establishes that Scopes had indeed taught evolution to his high school class. The state rests.

Darrow, with backing from the American Civil Liberties Union and the Baltimore *Sun* (through H.L. Mencken, the *Sun*'s star reporter, whose daily coverage of the trial help make it a national story), has paid the travel expenses for leading anthropologists, paleontologists, zoologists, and other scientists to Dayton to testify for the defense.

But Judge Raulston does not allow them to testify, ruling that their testimony would be irrelevant.

Darrow decides to call as his witness a man whose expertise with regard to the Bible is beyond question—and a man whom he knows the judge would not bar him from calling: William Jennings Bryan. This is perhaps the only instance in American history when a lawyer called opposing counsel as a witness at trial.

Bryan tries to use the opportunity to expound on his literal belief in every word in the King James Version of the Bible. But when pressed by Darrow, Bryan reveals an appallingly closed and uncurious mind: "I do not think about things that I do not think about." He also proclaims that he is more interested "in the Rock of Ages than in the age of rocks." He derides Darwin and his theories for suggesting that man had descended "not even from American monkeys, but Old World monkeys."

Bryan's demagoguery and literal belief in every word of the Bible leave him beaten and humiliated. His beliefs, as expounded in Dayton, seem silly. When they are challenged or questioned, he retreats into rote recitation of Biblical verses. Said Darrow:

"If today you can take a thing like evolution and make it a crime to teach it in the public school, tomorrow you can make it a crime to teach it in the private schools and then at the hustings or in church. At the next (legislative) session you may ban books and newspapers. If you can do one you can do the other and after a while, your honor, it is the setting of man against man, and creed against creed, until with flying banners and beating drums, we are marching backwards to the sixteenth century, when bigots lighted faggots to burn the men who dared to bring any intelligence and enlightenment and culture to the human mind."[5]

Although Scopes is convicted and fined $100, he wins his case on appeal. But Bryan's is lost. He dies in his sleep, probably from overeating in the Dayton heat, six days after the trial.

[4] 2000 population: 6,180. [5] Author's comment: Although this speech is not included in most collections of "Great Speeches of the 20th Century," I think it should be.

FIRST F.B.I. AGENT KILLED ON DUTY

OCTOBER 11, 1925. SPECIAL AGENT EDWIN C. SHANAHAN OF THE BUREAU OF INVESTIGATION, THE FORERUNNER OF THE F.B.I., IS SHOT AND KILLED BY AUTO THIEF MARTIN DURKIN. SHANAHAN IS THE FIRST AGENT TO BE KILLED IN THE LINE OF DUTY.

LET'S GO FOR A DRIVE

November 5, 1925. The Bronx River Parkway, which runs 13.2 miles from Yonkers to Valhalla, New York, is dedicated. It is the first highway in the nation designed to be driven slowly—the speed limit is still 40 m.p.h.—for pleasure driving, so that its beauty can be appreciated.

TENSION AND TURMOIL

TO THE MOON

March 16, 1926. Robert H. Goddard launches the first liquid-fueled rocket in Auburn, Massachusetts. The rocket, traveling at about 60 miles an hour, rises to a height of 41 feet in 2.5 seconds. Despite widespread derision— "To the *moon*? What are you, *nuts*?"—Goddard continues to launch bigger and more sophisticated rockets until his death in 1945. Goddard is considered the father of modern rocketry.

JUST ONE FOR ME, THANKS
1927. RAISINETTES ARE INTRODUCED.

FROM NEW YORK TO PARIS, SOLO, NON-STOP!

May 20, 1927. Airmail pilot Charles Augustus Lindbergh flies alone from New York to Paris. His plane, the *Spirit of St. Louis*, is loaded with 450 gallons of fuel. The flight from Roosevelt Field, near New York, takes Lindbergh 3,600 miles in thirty-three hours to Paris's Le Bourget airport. Lindbergh's flight captures the imagination of the world, and Lindbergh is hailed the world over as a hero. (A skilled pilot, he hates the nickname "Lucky Lindy.") President Coolidge dispatches the Navy cruiser *Memphis* to bring him and his plane home to America, and Coolidge greets him upon his arrival. Lindbergh is given a ticker tape parade in New York. The president presents Lindbergh with the Medal of Honor.

Lindbergh later marries Anne Morrow and they move to secluded Hopewell, New Jersey. There, at about 9 p.m. on March 1, 1932, their son Charles Jr. is kidnapped. The crime shocks the nation. A $50,000 ransom is demanded and paid. Charles A. Lindbergh Jr., age twenty months, appears on the cover of *Time* magazine on May 2, 1932—the youngest person ever to appear on *Time*'s cover. But the child had been killed. His decomposed body is found four and a half miles from his home on May 12, 1932, with a bullet hole in his skull.

Two years pass until a ten-dollar gold certificate, part of the ransom money, is passed at a bank in Manhattan. The police are notified, and on September 19, 1934, they arrest Bruno Richard Hauptmann, a carpenter from Germany. More ransom money is found on Hauptmann. Hauptmann is charged with murder and kidnapping for ransom.

Hauptmann vigorously denies his guilt. His trial lawyer was Edward J. "Deathhouse" Riley.[6] At trial, a wood expert links the wood in the homemade ladder used by the kidnapper to reach the child's bedroom window with wood found in Hauptmann's home. More Lindbergh ransom money is found in Hauptmann's closet. Hauptmann testifies at trial and continues to proclaim his innocence, but the jury does not believe him. He dies in New Jersey's electric chair on April 3, 1936. The executioner, hired by New Jersey for the special occasion, is Robert Elliott, the man who had performed the same grisly job on Sacco and Vanzetti in 1927 (see page 122).

[6] If you are a criminal defendant, you do not want your lawyer to be nicknamed "Deathhouse." It's like the nickname earned by pitcher Hugh Mulcahy, "Losing Pitcher." Or the nickname given to another pitcher, Walter Beck, "Boom-Boom," for the sound balls made bouncing off the outfield walls when he pitched.

MOUNT RUSHMORE

August 10, 1927. Work begins on South Dakota's Mt. Rushmore as a "national shrine." Idaho-born sculptor Gutzon Borglum drills six holes that day, to get the project started.

The monument consists of the faces of George Washington, Thomas Jefferson, Abraham Lincoln, and Theodore Roosevelt. Each face is approximately sixty feet high.

The project employs 400 local workers (paid up to $1.25 per hour) and blasts out nearly half a million tons of granite from the face of the mountain. No workers are killed during the fourteen years it takes to complete.

Borglum works on the mountain until his death on March 6, 1941. His son Lincoln finishes the project on October 31, 1941—the largest work of art on the planet.

THE CASE THAT WILL NOT DIE

August 23, 1927. Nicola Sacco, a shoe maker, and Bartolomeo Vanzetti, an eel monger, die in the Massachusetts electric chair. Sacco shouts "Long live anarchy!" Their trial, conviction (on July 24, 1921), and sentence for an April 15, 1920 payroll robbery at the Slater Morrill Shoe Company in South Braintree remains one of the most controversial and written-about cases in American history—*The Case That Will Not Die*, as Herbert Ehrmann, one of their lawyers, called it in his book. On August 23, 1977, Governor Michael Dukakis issues an apology on behalf of the State of Massachusetts and declares "Sacco and Vanzetti Memorial Day."

SIXTY HOME RUNS FOR BABE RUTH

SEPTEMBER 20, 1927. GEORGE HERMAN "BABE" RUTH HITS HIS SIXTIETH HOME RUN OF THE SEASON, A NUMBER PREVIOUSLY THOUGHT UNREACHABLE. HIS RECORD STANDS UNTIL OCTOBER 1, 1961 WHEN ROGER MARIS, ALSO OF THE YANKEES, HITS HIS SIXTY-FIRST HOMER ON THE LAST DAY OF THE SEASON.

BRRR

1928. The air conditioner, as we know it today, is developed for home use by Willis Haviland Carrier. He calls it the "Weathermaker." Homeowners, office workers, students, restaurateurs, and theatergoers breathe a collective sigh of relief.

GOLF, THE HARD WAY

1929. One of Al Capone's little-known talents was playing golf. Capone plays about twice a week. He frequently shoots in the low 80s, occasionally in the 70s. He plays with a group of 25 guarding him. Some of his guards carry Thompson submachine guns. His usual partner is Jack McGurn, nicknamed "Machine Gun." McGurn had planned the St. Valentine's Day massacre. Another golfing companion is Murray "The Camel" Humphreys, who carried his gun in a shoulder holster while he played. Talk about putting a crimp in your swing.

RAT-A-TAT-TAT

February 14, 1929. The St. Valentine's Day Massacre. Seven gangsters are mowed down by machine gun fire at the S.M.C. Cartage Company's garage at 2122 North Clark Street, in Chicago.

THE CRASH

October 24–29, 1929. The stock market crashes, or, as *Variety* puts it, "Wall Street Lays an Egg." Eleven important investors commit suicide. The market takes twenty-five years to recover. The full employment brought about after the United States enters World War II in December, 1941, as well as F.D.R.'s recovery policies, help pull the country out of the Great Depression.

HAPPY NEW YEAR!

December 31, 1929. When Guy Lombardo (born Gaetano Albert Lombardo) and his Royal Canadians, a famous dance band of the time, are hired to play at a New Year's Eve party at New York City's Roosevelt Hotel, a New Year's tradition is born. The band plays "Auld Lang Syne," a Scottish song first published in 1796, that night and every New Year's Eve through 1976. (Lombardo died in 1977.) The festivities and the song are heard on the radio, and later seen on television. Many people believe that the song is an ancient New Year's tradition. It is now.

IT HAS ITS UPS AND DOWNS

July 22, 1930. Pedro Flores obtains a trademark for the name "YO-YO." He later sells the name and his company to the Donald Duncan company.

YUM

1930. Ruth Wakefield invents the toll house chocolate-chip cookie

PAY YOUR TAXES!

October 18, 1931. Al Capone of Chicago and Cicero, Illinois, America's most notorious gangster, is convicted of federal income tax evasion. On November 24, he is sentenced to eleven years in prison and fined $50,000 plus $7,692 in court costs and $215,000 in back taxes, plus interest. Capone serves his time in the federal penitentiary in Atlanta and on Alcatraz, in San Francisco Bay. After seven and a half years in prison, he is released on November 16, 1939. He dies on January 25, 1947.

OH, TO BE 80

January 12, 1932. Justice Oliver Wendell Holmes Jr., a wounded Civil War veteran, retires from the Supreme Court of the United States after thirty years. At ninety, Holmes is the oldest justice in history.

THE BONUS ARMY

July 28, 1932. In 1924 Congress voted to give a bonus to each veteran of the Great War. (It was not called World War I yet. World War II is still nine years away.) $1.25 for each day overseas, plus $1 for each day served in the States. The bonus is to be paid in 1945.

In June, 1932, in the depths of the Depression, 15,000 veterans, most desperate and many destitute, and their families march on Washington, D.C., to demand that their promised bonuses be paid immediately.

On June 17, 1932, the United States Senate votes sixty-two to eighteen not to give the veterans their bonus immediately. The veterans, victorious in battle, but defeated by their own representatives, stay in Washington to continue their protest until Congress adjourns on July 17.

Washington police try to remove the marchers and their camps peacefully, but two people are killed. When President Herbert Hoover learns what has happened, he orders federal troops to disperse the marchers. They do. The troops, with cavalry and fixed bayonets, are directed by Army Chief of Staff Gen. Douglas MacArthur and Maj. Dwight D. Eisenhower. The troops and their six tanks are commanded by Gen. George S. Patton.

As though the Depression were not bad enough, the sight of the United States Army using tanks and mounted soldiers against unarmed veterans in the streets of the nation's capital is both depressing and unforgettable.

THE THIRD WINTER OLYMPICS IN LAKE PLACID, 1932

February 4, 1932. The third Winter Olympics are opened in Lake Placid, New York (population 2,600), by New York's governor, Franklin D. Roosevelt. Seventeen nations compete. Sled dog racing is a demonstration event. It does not catch on. Eddie Eagan, who had won a gold medal in light-heavyweight boxing in 1920, wins a gold medal in bobsleigh. He is still the only man to win golds in both Summer and Winter games.

THE NEW DEAL

July 2, 1932. After becoming the first person to fly to a convention to accept the nomination for president of the United States in person, Franklin Delano Roosevelt, the governor of New York, tells the Democratic convention in Chicago: "I pledge you, I pledge myself, to a new deal for the American people." The phrase "New Deal" is picked up by newspapers all across the country, and many of Roosevelt's policies are considered part of his "New Deal."

A REASON TO VISIT NORTH DAKOTA

July 14, 1932. The International Peace Garden is dedicated on the border between North Dakota, United States, and Manitoba, Canada. North Dakota becomes known as the "Peace Garden" state.

THE 1932 OLYMPICS IN LOS ANGELES

July 30, 1932. The tenth Olympic Games of the modern era are opened in Los Angeles by Vice President Charles Curtis. The games feature Mildred "Babe"—for Babe Ruth—Didrickson. In the first women's javelin event, Didrickson wins the gold. She also wins the gold medal in the first women's 80-meter hurdles. She would have won the gold in the high jump too, but her jumping style is ruled illegal, and she settles for the silver.

GUISEPPE ZANGARA

February 15, 1933. Bayfront Park, Miami. Five-foot tall Guiseppe Zangara, an immigrant bricklayer hit hard by the Depression (and suffering from chronic flatulence, although the connection between that condition and Zangara's subsequent behavior is hard to pinpoint) stands on a wobbly chair for a better view, pulls out his .32 pistol, and shoots at president-elect Franklin D. Roosevelt. But his aim is not very good, and, while Roosevelt is unharmed, Zangara shoots five others, including Chicago Mayor Anton Cermak, seated next to Roosevelt. Cermak says, "I'm glad it was me and not you, Mr. President."

When Cermak dies on March 6, Zangara is charged with murder. He is convicted and sentenced to death. He dies in Florida's electric chair on March 20, 1933.

THE ONLY THING WE HAVE TO FEAR IS FEAR ITSELF

March 4, 1933. Franklin Delano Roosevelt uses a number of memorable phrases in his first inaugural address as president of the United States. Among them: "Let me assert my firm belief that the only thing we have to fear is fear itself—nameless, unreasoning, unjustified terror which paralyzes needed efforts to convert retreat into advance."

MADAM SECRETARY

March 4, 1933. Francis Perkins becomes secretary of labor, a position she will hold for the twelve years of Franklin D. Roosevelt's administration. She is the first woman to serve in any president's cabinet.

GALLANT FOX WINS THE TRIPLE CROWN

Gallant Fox wins thoroughbred's Triple Crown with jockey Earle Sande up—the Kentucky Derby, the Preakness, and, on June 7, 1930, the Belmont by three lengths. Gallant Fox is the sire of Omaha, the 1935 Triple Crown winner.

THE XXTH AMENDMENT

January 23, 1933. The XXth Amendment to the Constitution of the United States is ratified, changing the date of the president's inauguration from March 4 to January 20. At his second inauguration in 1937, Franklin D. Roosevelt becomes the first president sworn in on January 20.

REPEAL!

December 5, 1933. The XXIst Amendment to the Constitution of the United States is ratified, repealing the XVIIIth Amendment. America's "noble experiment"—Prohibition—is over.

JEROME, MOSES, AND LOUIS

1934. Jerome Lester Horwitz, his brother Moses, and Louis Feinberg release their first film, a 19-minute short called "Women Haters." They are better known as Curly, Moe, and Larry—The Three Stooges. 96 other films and hilarity ensue.

ARMING F.B.I. AGENTS

June 18, 1934. Congress enacts legislation authorizing F.B.I. agents to make arrests and to carry firearms. Previously, they could only make citizen's arrests, and had to call on local police or U.S. Marshals to make an arrest.

THE WOMAN IN RED FINGERS PUBLIC ENEMY #1

June 22, 1934. John Dillinger, "Public Enemy #1," is fingered by the "Woman in Red"—his companion Ana Cumpanas. She wears a red dress as a prearranged tip-off for federal agents. Dillinger is shot and killed outside the Biograph Theater in Chicago. The movie playing is *Manhattan Melodrama*, starring Clark Gable, William Powell, Myrna Loy, and Mickey Rooney.

A.A. FOUNDED

June 10, 1935. After a series of bouts with alcohol, Bill Wilson finds a formula to help him and millions of others stay sober. As "Bill W." he founds Alcoholics Anonymous. Today, A.A. has meetings in over 150 countries.

THE F.B.I. IS BORN

July 1, 1935. The Department of Justice's Bureau of Investigation changes its name to the Federal Bureau of Investigation—the F.B.I. The F.B.I. becomes the most respected law enforcement agency in the world.

THE BIRTH OF THE TRAMPOLINE

1935. At the University of Iowa, in his garage, George Nissen invents the trampoline.

MONOPOLY

November 5, 1935. Monopoly, the board game that put Marvin Gardens, Atlantic Avenue, and Boardwalk on the national map, makes its debut.

SOCIAL SECURITY

AUGUST 14, 1935. PRESIDENT FRANKLIN D. ROOSEVELT SIGNS THE SOCIAL SECURITY ACT IN THE CABINET ROOM OF THE WHITE HOUSE.

I'LL TAKE ONE PLEASE

1936. The Tootsie Roll (in Spanish, "Rollo de Tootsie") is introduced.

THE AMAZING JESSE OWENS

August 3–9, 1936. Twenty-two-year-old Jesse Owens, an African-American from Oakville, Alabama, wins four gold medals at the 1936 Olympics in Berlin, Germany. German Chancellor Hitler staged the Olympics to proclaim what he believes is the superiority of the Aryan race to all others. Owens's four gold medals disprove that. Owens is triumphant in the 100-meter dash, the 200-meter dash, the 4x100-meter relay, and the long jump. His long jump mark of 26' 5" will stand for twenty-four years.

THE HINDENBURG

May 6, 1937. The hydrogen-filled German zeppelin Hindenburg, *the largest airship ever to fly, catches fire and explodes at 7:25 p.m. on live radio as it nears its mooring in Lakehurst, New Jersey, after a flight from Frankfurt-am-Main. Thirty-seven of the ship's seventy passengers die.*

THE OPENING OF THE GOLDEN GATE BRIDGE

May 28, 1937. By pressing a button at his desk in Washington, D.C., President Franklin D. Roosevelt officially opens the Golden Gate Bridge. The bridge connects San Francisco and Marin County. Taking four years to build and costing $35 million, the bridge is completed ahead of schedule and under budget. With a span of 4,200 feet, the Golden Gate Bridge is the longest suspension bridge in the world. Until the $325 million Verrazano Narrows Bridge connecting Brooklyn to Staten Island in New York City is opened on November 21, 1964. Its span is 4,260 feet. The stationery of the Golden Gate Bridge Authority had to be changed. It no longer proclaims the Golden Gate the "World's Longest" suspension bridge. After the Verrazano Narrows opens, the Golden Gate stationery says: "World's Greatest Suspension Bridge."

AMELIA EARHART VANISHES

July 2, 1937. America's most famous female aviator, Amelia Earhart, and navigator Fred Noonan disappear in her custom-built Lockheed 10E Electra while flying from New Guinea to Howland Island in the Pacific.

MR. JUSTICE HUGO BLACK AND THE K.K.K.

August 12, 1937. President Franklin D. Roosevelt nominates U.S. Senator Hugo Lafayette Black (D-Ala.), an enthusiastic supporter of Roosevelt's New Deal, to succeed Willis van Devanter on the Supreme Court of the United States—the first of F.D.R.'s nine Supreme Court appointments (second only to George Washington's eleven). Usually, when the nominee is a senator, confirmation is assured. And so it is with Black. He is confirmed by sixty-three to sixteen on August 17.

Shortly after he is sworn in as a justice, newspapers report Black's prior membership in the Robert E. Lee chapter of the Ku Klux Klan in Alabama. Black joined the Klan on September 13, 1923, and participated in a few K.K.K. parades and speeches. He resigned from the Klan in 1925.

Black addresses the nation on the radio on October 1, 1937—a unique event for a Supreme Court justice, even a new one. He states that he had joined the Klan to help him in politics, that he does not adhere to its views, and does not consider himself a Klansman.

Black serves on the Court for thirty-four years until his resignation in 1971. At the time, he is recognized as one of the great justices of all time—a true champion of individual rights, freedom, and liberties. He carries a copy of the Constitution in his pocket.

The joke was told about Black and his colleague, Justice William O. Douglas, chuckling about "strict constructionists," a phrase used mostly by Nixon Republicans to define "law and order" conservative judges. Black and Douglas, who championed the 1st Amendment, are said to have told each other: "They're talking about us."

SOME DAY, HER PRINCE WILL COME
December 21, 1937. Opening night for Walt Disney's *Snow White and the Seven Dwarfs*. This is the first animated full-length feature film ever released in America.

THE WORLD NEWS ROUNDUP
March 13, 1938. Robert Trout is the host as "The C.B.S. World News Roundup" debuts on the radio. The broadcast includes shortwave broadcasts from Paris, Berlin, Rome, London, and Vienna.

LOUIS VS. SCHMELING BEFORE 70,000 AND MILLIONS MORE ON THE RADIO

June 22, 1938. The place: Yankee Stadium. (The Yankees were in Cleveland, in the midst of a fourteen-game road trip.) The event: the fight for the heavyweight championship of the world, one of the stellar sporting events of the century. Joe Louis, twenty-four, "The Brown Bomber," a black man from Detroit, Michigan, U.S.A., vs. Max Schmeling, thirty-two, from Brandenburg, Germany. Schmeling had become champion, briefly, by beating Jack Sharkey on June 13, 1930.

Adolf Hitler had touted the superiority of the Aryan race. Schmeling was the embodiment of that philosophy (although he was probably neither a Nazi nor a Nazi sympathizer[7]; and he had black hair). One of Schmeling's entourage proclaimed that he would use the purse from the fight, which Schmeling would of course win, to help Germany build more tanks.

Louis and Schmeling had fought before. On June 12, 1936, Schmeling had knocked out Louis in the twelfth round—up to that time, Louis's only loss as a pro. Since then, Louis had become champion (on June 22, 1937, by knocking out James Braddock), but he did not consider himself the real champion until he avenged his previous loss to Schmeling.

The 70,000 fans at Yankee Stadium are still getting seated when Louis destroys Schmeling in the first round. Schmeling throws just two punches.

The match lasts just two minutes and four seconds. "Schmeling is down," in the words of broadcaster Clem McCarthy. Schmeling's corner men throw in the towel, and the fight is over.

Joe Louis becomes one of the first black men to be hailed as a true American sports hero. As sportswriter Jimmy Cannon wrote about Louis, "He is a credit to his race—the human race."

[7] One of Schmeling's American managers is Joe Jacobs, who is Jewish. Jacobs became immortalized for two quotes, which appear in Bartlett's *Familiar Quotations*: After Schmeling's loss in a rematch with Jack Sharkey in 1932: "We wuz robbed." And later, after he got out of a sick bed to see the first game of the 1935 World Series, "I should have stood in bed."

THE BROADCAST THAT SCARED AMERICA

October 30, 1938. Orson Welles's "Mercury Theater" broadcasts a pre-Halloween radio adaptation of H.G. Wells's classic science fiction novel, *The War of the Worlds.*

Millions of Americans tune in to hear what sounds like real reporters and citizens describing the invasion of giant Martian beings in "Grovers Mill, New Jersey." But listeners to other radio stations hear the usual music programming. Nevertheless, millions of Americans are scared to death, and Welles is forced to apologize.

MARIAN ANDERSON

Early in 1939, opera singer Marian Anderson, a contralto, is denied the opportunity to sing at Constitution Hall in Washington, D.C. The Daughters of the American Revolution, which own Constitution Hall, won't let Anderson sing there because she is black.

First Lady Eleanor Roosevelt, a member of the D.A.R., resigns from the organization and offers Anderson the opportunity to sing in front of the Lincoln Memorial. Anderson accepts, and on Easter Sunday, April 9, 1939, she sings there before a crowd of 75,000—the largest crowd ever to hear a concert at the Memorial—and a radio audience of millions. Anderson sings "America," "Ave Maria," "Gospel Train," "Trampin'," "My Soul Is Anchored in the Lord," and "Nobody Knows the Trouble I've Seen."

WILLIAM O. DOUGLAS

March 20, 1939. William O. Douglas is nominated by President Franklin D. Roosevelt to serve as an associate justice of the Supreme Court. Douglas is forty years old, the second youngest ever appointed. (Joseph Story, appointed in 1811, was thirty-two.) A staunch defender of the Bill of Rights, Douglas—who has parallel careers as a traveler, hiker, environmentalist, and author— serves on the Court longer than anyone in history, retiring on November 12, 1975, after thirty-six years.

THE HALL OF FAME OPENS

June 12, 1939. The National Baseball Hall of Fame and Museum opens in Cooperstown, New York—America's first Hall of Fame. The first five inductees are Christy Mathewson, Babe Ruth, Ty Cobb, Walter Johnson, and Honus Wagner. Today, they are represented in the five stars of the Hall's logo.

G.W.T.W.

December 15, 1939. *Gone With the Wind* opens in Atlanta, where much of the film is set. Producer David O. Selznick paid the novel's author, Margaret Mitchell, an unprecedented $50,000 for the film rights. The movie is nominated for thirteen Oscars and wins eight.

AN OSCAR FOR HATTIE McDANIEL

February 29, 1940. Hattie McDaniel wins an Oscar for best supporting actress for her portrayal of "Mammy" in *Gone With the Wind*, the first black actor or actress to win an Academy Award. It will be another twenty-four years until a black man wins an Oscar as best actor in a starring role—April 13, 1964, when Sidney Poitier, who played "Homer Smith," wins for *Lillies of the Field*.

McDaniel is criticized for playing maids and other menial roles—usually the only roles available at the time for a black woman. Says McDaniel: "I'd rather *play* a maid than *be* one."

THE PLEDGE OF ALLEGIANCE

September 7, 1892. The U.S. Pledge of Allegiance, by Francis Bellamy, is published in *Youth's Companion*, a children's magazine. The phrase "under God" is added to the pledge by act of Congress on Flag Day, June 14, 1954.

April 25, 1940. The Supreme Court of the United States rules that requiring all pupils in a public school to salute the American flag and recite the Pledge of Allegiance does not constitute an establishment of religion, prohibited by the First Amendment.

Lillian and William Gobitis, Jehovah's Witnesses, sue on behalf of their children. They believe that saluting the flag is akin to having a "graven image," which the Second Commandment prohibits, or having other gods, prohibited by the First Commandment. But by an eight to one majority in *Minersville School District v. Gobitis*, the Court upholds the requirement of the compulsory flag salute.

On June 14, 1943, in the middle of World War II, the Court reconsiders and reaches a different conclusion. In *West Virginia State Board of Education v. Barnette,* the Court rules that "compulsory unification of opinion" is prohibited by the First Amendment. As Justice Robert Jackson writes, "If there is any fixed star in our constitutional constellation, it is that no official high or petty can prescribe what shall be orthodox in politics, nationalism, religion, or other matters of opinion, or force citizens to confess by word or act their faith therein."

F.D.R.'S THIRD TERM

November 5, 1940. Franklin Delano Roosevelt, Democrat of New York, is elected to a third term as president of the United States—the first man to serve more than two terms. He defeats Republican Wendell Willkie, a Wall Street lawyer from New York who had been a Roosevelt delegate in 1932. Willkie never held public office. (The last president who never held elective office was Herbert Hoover.)

JOE D

Between May 15 and July 16, 1941, many Americans woke up asking the same question: "How'd Joe do?" Joe is New York Yankee slugger Joe DiMaggio. During that span, DiMaggio hits in fifty-six straight games—a record that still stands. No other player has come within ten of DiMaggio's streak.

PEARL HARBOR DAY

December 7, 1941, 7:53 a.m. Planes from Japanese aircraft carriers 247 miles away attack the United States naval base at Pearl Harbor on the island of Oahu in the Hawaiian Islands. The surprise attack leaves 2,403 dead and 188 American planes destroyed—many on the ground. The battleship *Arizona* sinks with 1,300 sailors lost. The attack plunges the United States into the War.

"A DAY WHICH WILL LIVE IN INFAMY"

December 8, 1941. Before a joint session of Congress, President Franklin D. Roosevelt declares December 7 "a day which will live in infamy." He asks for and gets a declaration of war against Japan.

THE INFAMOUS EXECUTIVE ORDER 9066

February 19, 1942. President Franklin D. Roosevelt signs Executive Order 9066 authorizing the United States military to round up and intern 110,000 American citizens of Japanese ancestry. No similar detention order is issued involving Italian-Americans or German-Americans, although the United States is at war with Italy and Germany as well as with Japan. Many of these Japanese-Americans—American citizens—were born in the United States.

The final exclusion order is issued on April 30, 1942. The internees are held in ten "relocation centers" in remote, inland areas: Poston and Gila River, Arizona; Rohwer and Jerome, Arkansas; Tule Lake and Manzanar, California; Amache, Colorado; Minidoka, Idaho; Topaz, Utah; and Heart Mountain, Wyoming.

The move has the enthusiastic support of California's Republican Attorney General, Earl Warren. This is a significant blot on the record of Warren, who, as Chief Justice of the United States 1953–1969, becomes a champion of individual rights and liberties. The Nisei (i.e., American citizens of Japanese ancestry) are allowed to bring two suitcases with them. Property has to be sold (usually at a loss) within hours. Most lose their homes, farms, stores—everything.

Some 17,000 Japanese-Americans enlist in the U.S. military. The 442nd Regimental "Go For Broke" Combat Team, made up primarily of Japanese-Americans, becomes the most decorated military unit in the U.S. Army.

It was not until 1988 that the United States government recognized the injustice that had been done to these American citizens and their families, and the stain that had been put on America's reputation. A sum of $20,000 was awarded to each of the 60,000 survivors of the camps.

THE DOOLITTLE RAID

April 18, 1942. Led by Lt. Col. James H. Doolittle, 16 B-25s take off from the U.S.S. *Hornet* to bomb Toyko. Just four months after the Japanese attack on Pearl Harbor, the American bombing of the Japanese capital—which the Japanese government had assured its people was impossible—is an incredible boost for sagging American morale.

U.S. INVADED!

June 6–7, 1942. The United States is invaded for the first time since the War of 1812, as Japanese troops occupy Kiska and Attu in the Aleutian Islands of Alaska. Attu is recaptured on May 11, 1943, but at a high cost: 3,900 American casualties, including 549 killed. Some 2,300 Japanese soldiers are killed, and only 28 are captured—none of them officers. On August 7, 1943, 34,000 U.S. troops and 5,300 Canadians retake Kiska, but it had been abandoned by the Japanese.

GERMAN SABOTEURS CAUGHT, TRIED, AND EXECUTED

June 13, 1942. German submarine U-202 surfaces off the coast of Long Island, near New York City. Four German would-be saboteurs, armed with primers, explosives, incendiaries, and American cash, land on the beach.

On June 17, another group of four German would-be saboteurs lands on Ponte Vedra Beach in Florida, put ashore by another U-boat, U-584.

But by June 27, 1942, all eight have been captured by the F.B.I. They are tried July 8–August 4 by a Military Commission composed of seven U.S. Army officers. All are convicted of espionage. Six are sentenced to death and are executed on August 8. One is sentenced to life imprisonment, and one to thirty years.

THE BATTLE OF MIDWAY

June 4, 1942. The Battle of Midway. A speck of land less than four miles long about a third of the way from Hawaii to Japan, Midway became the most important spot in the world when naval forces from the United States and Japan meet for what proves to be the crucial naval battle of World War II. The Japanese fleet consists of forty-five destroyers, eleven battleships, thirteen cruisers, and six aircraft carriers. The Americans use three aircraft carriers, eight cruisers, and fourteen destroyers. After Midway, there is little the Japanese Navy can do besides be on the defensive.

FIRST SHELLING OF A U.S. MILITARY BASE SINCE 1812

June 21, 1942. Ft. Stevens, Oregon, a U.S. Army post by the mouth of the Columbia River, is shelled by seventeen rounds fired by Japanese submarine I-25. This is the first attack on a U.S. mainland military post since the War of 1812. The attack does no serious damage.

SURGERY UNDER THE SEA

September 11, 1942. Nineteen-year-old Dean Rector of the U.S. Navy has appendicitis. If his appendix is not removed, and removed soon, he will die. But he can't get to a doctor. In fact, the nearest Navy surgeon is about 2,000 miles away. Rector is on the submarine Seadragon 120 feet below the surface of the South

China Sea, with enemy ships above. Who will operate? 23-year-old Chief Pharmacist's Mate Wheeler "Johnny" Lipes. Lipes has seen one or two appendectomies during his training, and he has a book which details the operation.

Wearing reversed pajama tops as surgical gowns, and using a gauze-covered tea strainer to administer ether, the jerry-rigged medical team begins the operation on the table in the sub's wardroom. For retractors, "Doc" Lipes uses bent spoons. The operation, which usually takes 45 minutes, takes two and a half hours. Rector makes a full recovery. His appendix is preserved in a bottle.

THE SULLIVANS

November 14, 1942. The U.S. light cruiser *Juneau* is sunk near Guadalcanal in the Pacific. On board are Albert, Francis, George, Joseph, and Madison Sullivan, five brothers, of Waterloo, Iowa. All five are lost. The movie *The Fighting Sullivans*, with Anne Baxter, Thomas Mitchell, and Ward Bond, is released in 1944, and the navy destroyer *The Sullivans* is launched in September, 1943.

THE FIRST NUCLEAR REACTOR

December 2, 1942. At a squash court at the University of Chicago, Enrico Fermi designs and creates the world's first artificial nuclear reactor. Fermi is one of the few scientists to have an element named for him—Fermium, element #100.

PREPARE TO BOARD: THE JOURNEY OF U-505

On June 4, 1944 nine sailors from the U.S.S. *Pillsbury* do something that American sailors had not done for many years: off the west coast of Africa, they board an enemy ship on the high seas. The enemy ship: a German type IX-C submarine, U-505.

The American ships *Guadalcanal*, *Pope*, *Flaherty*, *Pillsbury*, *Chatelain*, and *Jenks*, part of Task Group 22.3, had dropped depth charges to force the sub to surface. Her crew surrenders and is picked up by the *Jenks* and the *Chatelain*. They are imprisoned separately from other P.O.W.s, lest word of the U-505's capture leak back to Germany. The story of her capture is not made public until after Germany surrendered. Families of U-505's crew are informed that their loved ones are dead, as U-505 was thought to have perished.

Under the command of Chicago native Captain Daniel Gallery, the men of the *Pillsbury* had trained to prevent the sub from being scuttled or blown up. They had also trained to find and recover the ship's code books and top secret code device—the Ultra machine. The ship is secured, although partially submerged, and towed over 2,000 miles—the longest towing operation of the war—to a secret berth in Bermuda.

After the war, the ship is towed once again from Bermuda north to Portsmouth, New Hampshire.

Starting on May 15, 1954, U-505 is towed an additional 3,000 miles through the twenty-eight locks of the St. Lawrence Seaway, through four of the Great Lakes to Lake Michigan. The people of Chicago raise $250,000 to bring the ship to Chicago and install her at the Museum of Science and Industry. The ship weighs 750 tons and is 252 feet long. She arrives in Chicago by barge from nearby Gary, Indiana, on June 26, 1954. Railroad tracks have been laid for the trip from Lake Michigan 800 feet across Lake Shore Drive (the signs proclaim "Submarine Crossing") to the museum a week later, where it becomes a permanent exhibit—the museum's most popular. On September 25, 1954, the ship is dedicated as a National Historic Landmark, the only U-boat on display in a museum.

THE DOLL LADY

August 14, 1944. Velvalee Dickinson, a Sacramento native and Stanford graduate, owns a doll store on Madison Avenue in New York. But she has another occupation as well. She is a spy for Japan. On this date, she is sentenced upon her guilty plea to espionage.

"The Doll Lady" sent messages about U.S. Navy ships inside dolls, which she shipped to Buenos Aires, Argentina, where they were forwarded to Japan. "The Doll Lady" got ten years in federal prison—the maximum.

HERE'S DICK TRACY

1945. During a newspaper strike, New York City Mayor Fiorello LaGuardia reads the funnies on W.N.Y.C., the city's radio station.

THE FLAG-RAISING ON IWO JIMA

February 23, 1945. The American flag is raised on Mt. Surabachi on the Pacific Island of Iwo Jima. Joe Rosentha's photograph of the event is the most duplicated photo of the war.

F.D.R. DIES. H.S.T. SWORN IN

April 12, 1945. At his vacation home in Warm Springs, Georgia, Franklin Delano Roosevelt dies after twelve years as president. After only eighty-two days as vice president, Harry S. Truman of Missouri is sworn in as president at 7:09 p.m. by Chief Justice Harlan F. Stone at the White House. The next day, he explains to reporters how he feels: "Boys, if you ever pray, pray for me now. I don't know if you fellows ever had a load of hay fall on you, but when they told me yesterday what had happened, I felt like the moon, the stars, and all the planets had fallen on me."

V.E. DAY

May 8, 1945. "V.E. Day"—Victory in Europe Day.

PLANE CRASHES INTO THE EMPIRE STATE BUILDING

July 28, 1945. A U.S. Army B-25 piloted by Lt. Colonel William Smith crashes into the 78th floor of the Empire State Building in New York City, killing fourteen office workers and three on board.

V.J. DAY

AUGUST 15, 1945. "V.J. DAY"—VICTORY OVER JAPAN DAY. EMPEROR HIROHITO SPEAKS TO HIS PEOPLE ON THE RADIO AT NOON TO ANNOUNCE HIS GOVERNMENT'S UNCONDITIONAL SURRENDER. IT IS THE FIRST TIME HIS PEOPLE HAVE HEARD HIS VOICE.

JAPAN SURRENDERS

September 2, 1945, 9 a.m. On the deck of the U.S. battleship *Missouri* in Tokyo Bay, Japan formally surrenders to the Allies, marking the end of World War II. Accompanying Supreme Commander for the Allied Powers Douglas MacArthur are Brig. Gen. Jonathan Wainwright, who had commanded U.S. troops at the surrender of Corregidor in the Philippines in 1942, and Lt. Gen. Arthur Percival, who commanded British troops at the fall of Singapore, also in 1942. From Tokyo Bay, Gen. Wainright proceeds to the Philippines to accept the Japanese surrender there.

Gen. Wainwright had been held by the Japanese as a prisoner of war from May 6, 1942 to August 25, 1945. Despite the opposition of Gen. MacArthur, who considers him a coward, President Harry S. Truman presents Gen. Wainwright with the Medal of Honor in the Rose Garden of the White House on September 10, 1945.

THE BIRTH OF THE U.N.

OCTOBER 24, 1945. THE UNITED NATIONS, MADE UP PRIMARILY OF GERMANY'S FIFTY-ONE ENEMIES OF WORLD WAR II, IS BORN IN SAN FRANCISCO, CALIFORNIA.

THE BALLPOINT PEN
October 30, 1945. The ballpoint goes on sale in New York for $12.50.

THE MANHATTAN PROJECT

The Manhattan Project is the ultra-secret American, British, and Canadian plan to build, test, and ultimately deliver an atomic bomb during World War II—and before Nazi Germany can do the same.

The project eventually employs over 130 people and costs nearly two billion dollars, spread over thirty institutions. Gen. Leslie Groves is the military leader, but physicist J. Robert Oppenheimer is the driving force behind the scientists who live and work in secluded Alamogordo and Los Alamos, New Mexico.

The project is so secret that even Harry S. Truman, vice president of the United States, is not informed until he becomes president upon Franklin Roosevelt's death.

On July 16, 1945, the first nuclear device, "Gadget," is successfully tested in the New Mexico desert. After that, work continues to turn the device into a bomb to be dropped from a plane.

The decision to drop the bomb on Japan is made by President Truman. His military advisors tell him that *without* the bomb, the invasion would be "another Okinawa," where 48,000 Americans died. Plans are readied to land 767,000 Marines and soldiers on Kyushu in "Operation Olympic." Untold hundreds of thousands of Americans and Japanese will die if the operation is carried out.

Truman gives the order. He believes—correctly, as it turned out—that despite its devastation, the bomb will lead to a quick end to the war.

Under secret orders, the U.S.S. *Indianapolis* had delivered "Little Boy," the first atomic bomb to be used in combat, to the 509 Composite Group on the island of Tinian, a thirty-nine-square-mile dot near Saipan in the Marianas. On July 29, on its return trip, the *Indianapolis* is sunk by a Japanese submarine and 881 crewmen are lost. Survivors are adrift in shark-infested waters for two days before anybody notices that the *Indianapolis* is missing.

Tinian is six hours' flying time from Japan. During the War, Tinian becomes the busiest airbase in the world. The bomb is loaded into the bomb bay of a B-29 called "Enola Gay," named for pilot Paul Tibbets's mother. The dropping of the bomb on Hiroshima, Japan, on August 6, 1945, changes the world, literally in an instant. Some 70,000 people and sixty percent of the city are vaporized, and by December, 140,000 have died from the after-effects of the nuclear bombing.

Later that day, Truman addresses the nation and the world on the radio, saying "The force from which the sun draws its power has been used against those who brought war to the Far East."

But the Japanese do not surrender. Truman threatens a "rain of ruin" on Japan. Leaflets are dropped on Japan on August 8 demanding unconditional surrender. Nothing else will be accepted. But still—no surrender. So, on August 9, a B-29 called "Bockscar," piloted by Major Charles W. Sweeney, carries a second nuclear bomb, "Fat Man," to Nagasaki. Some 20,000 die instantly.

TRUMAN REDESIGNS THE GREAT SEAL OF THE UNITED STATES

October 26, 1945. The Seal of the United States, in use since Rutherford B. Hayes's administration in 1880, is redesigned by President Harry S. Truman. He turns the eagle to face the olive branch rather than war arrows held in its talons.

DR. SPOCK

July 14, 1946. *The Common Sense Book of Baby and Child Care*, by Benjamin Spock, M.D., one of the best-selling books of all time, is published. It has sold over fifty million copies in eight editions, and has been translated into thirty-nine languages.

CHARGE IT

1946. The first bank to issue a credit card is Brooklyn, New York's Flatbush National Bank. It was invented by John Biggins. Diners Club issues its first card (actually a charge card) in 1950. In 1958, American Express and Bank of America (later Visa) issue their first credit cards.

FIRST STATE OF THE UNION TO BE BROADCAST

JANUARY 6, 1947, 1 P.M. PRESIDENT HARRY S. TRUMAN
DELIVERS THE FIRST STATE OF THE UNION ADDRESS,
MANDATED BY ARTICLE II SECTION III OF THE CONSTITUTION
OF THE UNITED STATES, TO BE BROADCAST ON RADIO.

THE COMING OF JACKIE ROBINSON

April 15, 1947. Jack Roosevelt Robinson makes his debut
with the Brooklyn Dodgers—the first black man to play major
league baseball in the modern era. Signed by Dodgers' owner
Branch Rickey, Robinson had to promise Rickey that he would
not react to racial insults and taunts on the field for a year—
that he would not fight back. Robinson let his bat, his glove,
his feet, and his winning attitude—particularly his daring
baserunning—talk for him. Owners who were against breaking
baseball's unwritten color line soon noticed two things about
Robinson and the Dodgers. They drew lots of fans. And they
won. Between 1947 and 1956, the Brooklyn Dodgers won the
National League pennant six times.

There were better players than Robinson in the Negro Leagues, which Rickey had Clyde Sukeforth secretly scout for him. Satchell Page, Josh Gibson, Judy Johnson, and Cool Papa Bell were established stars of the Negro Leagues. But Rickey was looking for somebody younger. In Robinson—only twenty-eight—he also found a player who was a college man (three years at U.C.L.A.) and a man who had been an officer—a Lieutenant—in the U.S. Army. Rickey thought that Robinson would command some respect.

On June 5, 1947, Larry Doby breaks the color line in the American League for Cleveland Indians owner Bill Veeck. Years later, Robinson, Doby, Rickey, and Veeck are all elected to baseball's Hall of Fame in Cooperstown, New York.

THE TAFT-HARTLEY ACT

June 20, 1947. President Harry Truman vetoes the Taft-Hartley Labor Act—authorizing a government-imposed 80-day cooling off period—but his veto is overridden, and the law is enacted.

CHUCK YEAGER BREAKS THE SOUND BARRIER

October 14, 1947. Col. Chuck Yeager, said to have 20/10 vision, breaks the sound barrier in level flight, piloting the Bell X-1. Yeager nicknames his bright orange rocket plane *Glamorous Glennis*, after his wife.

HERE'S THE PICTURE

1948. The Polaroid camera hits the market, invented by Dr. Edwin Land. Only Thomas Edison has more patents.

THE ALGER HISS CASE

August 3, 1948. Whittaker Chambers, a former member of the Communist Party, testifies in secret before the House Committee on Un-American Activities. He claims that Alger Hiss had been a member of the Communist Party. Hiss, a graduate of Harvard Law School and a former law clerk for Justice Oliver Wendell Holmes Jr., is a high official of the United States Department of State, and later serves as president of the Carnegie Endowment.

Hiss testifies before the Committee, denies the charges, and claims never to have met Chambers. The Committee appoints a subcommittee and names an obscure Republican Congressman from California, one Richard M. Nixon, as its chairman.

Hiss repeats under oath that he was never a Communist, and that when he met a man he later identified as Chambers, Chambers was using a different name.

Chambers claims that Hiss gave him confidential State Department documents. Hiss, under oath, again denies the charges. Hiss is charged with perjury and goes to trial. The jury deadlocks and a mistrial is declared. At the second trial, Hiss is convicted of perjury and sentenced to five years.

The case becomes a springboard for the political career of Richard Nixon, who rides the Hiss case to the United States Senate, and then, in 1952 and again in 1956, to a spot on the Republican national ticket with Dwight D. Eisenhower.

Only two men have appeared on the national ticket five times: Franklin D. Roosevelt, as vice presidential candidate in 1920 with James Cox, and as presidential candidate in 1932, 1936, 1940, and 1944; and Nixon, as vice presidential candidate in 1952 and 1956, and as presidential candidate in 1960, 1968, and 1972.

The Republicans blame Hiss and the Democrats for everything they can think of and ride Dwight D. Eisenhower's coattails to the White House in 1952, singing "I Like Ike."

TRUMAN DESEGREGATES THE U.S. MILITARY
JULY 26, 1948. PRESIDENT HARRY S. TRUMAN ISSUES AN EXECUTIVE ORDER DESEGREGATING AMERICAN ARMED FORCES.

THE BERLIN AIRLIFT

June 24, 1948–May 11, 1949. When the Soviets block rail and car access to West Berlin, the United States, aided by Great Britain, institutes an airlift to the beleaguered city. Nicknamed "Operation Vittles," the airlift flies 278,228 flights into Berlin, bringing in 2,326,406 tons of food and 1.5 million tons of coal. Berlin, a free city in the midst of Communist-controlled East Germany, will not be abandoned. Even after the Soviets relent and permit rail and truck traffic through East Berlin (which they controlled) to continue to West Berlin, the flights continue until Berlin has stockpiled supplies in case of a future blockade.

CITATION WINS THE TRIPLE CROWN

Citation wins thoroughbred's Triple Crown, with jockey Eddie Arcaro winning the Kentucky Derby, the Preakness, and, on June 12, 1948, the Belmont Stakes.

GOOD OLE JOE EARLEY NIGHT

September 28, 1948. In a publicity stunt for the ages, Cleveland Indians' owner Bill Veeck stages a "Salute to Good Ole Joe Earley" night. Earley, twenty-eight, is a night watchman at a car factory. He is a regular fan who complained that there were too many "nights" for players and none for the regular fans.

The date is set for the Indians' last home game of the season. Over 60,000 fans come to the stadium. Veeck charters a plane to fly in orchids from Hawaii for the first 20,000 female fans.

Veeck, the greatest promoter and showman in the history of baseball, gives Earley a new house and a car. Unfortunately, it was an outhouse and a jalopy. Among the other "gifts" for Early are chickens, goats, and pigs. After the gag gifts, he is given new appliances, luggage, a new convertible, and a lifetime American League pass.

The odd promotion must have helped. The Indians go on to win the American League pennant that year, then beat the Boston Braves in the World Series.

THE WRONGEST HEADLINE EVER

November 2, 1948. The Chicago *Daily Tribune*, hoping to scoop the other newspapers, prints its front page a little early and a little wrong. The headline *had* to be right. All the polls said so: "DEWEY DEFEATS TRUMAN!" There's a famous photo of a beaming Harry S. Truman, just elected to a full four-year term in his own right, holding up the front page.

TRUMAN SWORN IN ON HIS OWN

January 20, 1949. After succeeding to the presidency upon the death of Franklin D. Roosevelt, Harry S. Truman is sworn in for four years, having been elected in his own right. Truman's is the first televised inauguration. Truman's Bible is opened to the Sermon on the Mount and the Ten Commandments.

AXIS SALLY

March 8, 1949. After a trial in Washington, D.C., Mildred Gillars (Mildred Elizabeth Sisk) is convicted of treason against the United States. Before World War II, the Portland, Maine, native was studying in Germany, and fell in love with her music professor. She wound up doing propaganda broadcasts for Radio Berlin. On the air, she was known as "Axis Sally," the European counterpart to Tokyo Rose (see page 162).

She is sentenced to ten to thirty years in prison. Upon her release, in 1962, she becomes a music teacher in Columbus, Ohio. She dies in 1988.

TOKYO ROSE

July 5, 1949. The most expensive trial (up to that time) in American history commences at the federal courthouse in San Francisco. The defendant: Iva Toguri D'Aquino. She was born in Los Angeles, California, and studied zoology at U.C.L.A. In 1941, she went to visit relatives in Japan. Once the war broke out on December 7, she was trapped in Japan. She did not speak Japanese. But her spoken English was good enough to get her a job broadcasting on Radio Tokyo. Her music-filled broadcasts were aimed at American and Allied soldiers and sailors in the Pacific. She tried to lower their morale by telling them that they were losing the war, that their wives had left them, and that their other ships had all been sunk by the Japanese. The Allied sailors gave her a nickname—"Tokyo Rose."

After the Japanese surrendered, she was charged with giving aid and comfort to the enemy in wartime—treason, the only crime defined in the Constitution (Article III, Section 3). To support the eight counts of treason, the government calls forty-six witnesses at the trial. D'Aquino is convicted on one count on September 29, 1949, and sentenced to ten years in prison. She serves just over six years, and is released in 1956.

On January 19, 1977, his last day in office, President Gerald R. Ford, a former Lt. Commander in the United States Navy who had served in the Pacific, pardons her without comment.

WORLD'S LARGEST CATSUP BOTTLE

OCTOBER, 1949. THE WORLD'S LARGEST CATSUP BOTTLE IS ERECTED FOR THE BOTTLING PLANT OF THE G.S. SUPPIGER CATSUP COMPANY, MAKERS OF BROOKS CATSUP, AS A WATER TOWER NEXT TO ROUTE 159, SOUTH OF COLLINSVILLE, ILLINOIS. IT IS SAVED FROM DEMOLITION AND LOVINGLY RESTORED IN 1995.

IN 2002 IT IS ADDED TO THE NATIONAL REGISTER OF HISTORIC PLACES. SURPRISINGLY, IT IS THE ONLY CATSUP BOTTLE ON THE LIST OF 85,014 SUCH SITES.

Chapter 5

Persecution and Protest

1950–1999

"Liberty and Union, now and forever, one and inseparable!"

Daniel Webster, January 26, 1830

SILLY PUTTY

February, 1950. Peter Hodgson Sr., a marketing consultant, borrows $147 to purchase a batch of silicone goo—a solid liquid. He places one-ounce gobs of the stuff in plastic eggs, calls it "Silly Putty," sells it for one dollar, and becomes a millionaire. By 1987, over two million Silly Putty eggs are sold annually. In 2000, the Smithsonian acquires two Silly Putty eggs for its exhibit on American "culture" of the 1950s.

POINT OF ORDER!

On February 9, 1950, during a speech in Wheeling, West Virginia, ostensibly celebrating Abraham Lincoln's birthday, Republican Joseph McCarthy, the junior United States senator from Wisconsin, proclaims that ours is a "Christian world," pitted against the atheistic Communist world. "Today," he says, "we are engaged in a final, all-out battle between communistic atheism and Christianity." While he waves a piece of paper, which, as usual, he never makes public, he shouts, "I have here in my hand a list...a list of names that were made known to the secretary of state as being members of the Communist Party and who nevertheless are still working and shaping policy in the State Department."

"I have in my hand a list!" becomes a typical McCarthy tactic—vitriolic, accusatory, unverifiable, but damning nonetheless.

This was the opening salvo in a battle which pitted Sen. McCarthy and his anti-Communist, flag-waving, fact-deprived attack-everyone zealots, to whom truth and justice meant very little, against the forces of reason, truth, and Constitutional protection.

The Senator gave his name to an era (roughly 1950–56) and a phenomenon: McCarthyism. Making outrageous statements, not backed up by any facts or evidence; accusing anybody who opposed his methods of being 1) a Communist, 2) a Communist sympathizer, or 3) a disloyal Communist dupe.

Just to be questioned by Sen. McCarthy, or called before his Senate Permanent Subcommittee on Investigations, meant the end of your career. To be thought of as having signed a petition, or even sharing a name with somebody who is on a list of something which a McCarthy crony didn't like—again, your career was over. People are blacklisted. Their calls aren't returned. Their friends shun them. Many in Hollywood cannot find work under their own names. A number of writing Oscars go unclaimed: the movies were written by blacklisted writers, using pseudonyms.

Sen. McCarthy is parodied by screenwriter George Axelrod in John Frankenheimer's 1962 film, *The Manchurian Candidate*, when the McCarthy-like character "Senator John Yerkes Iselin" asks his wife (Angela Lansbury) to give him a nice easy number he can remember—how many Communists *are* there in the state department? Mrs. Iselin looks at the bottle of Heinz ketchup in Iselin's hand and says: "Fifty-seven."

Sen. McCarthy ultimately took on the U.S. Army. The Army had refused to give G. David Schine, one of McCarthy's aides, special treatment. The Army–McCarthy hearings are televised coast-to-coast April 22–June 17, 1954. This is the first time that many Americans have seen Sen. McCarthy live, in full demonic dudgeon.

In one of the most courageous moments in the history of television, C.B.S.'s Edward R. Murrow, who was and still is the nation's most respected broadcast journalist, and his producer Fred W. Friendly air a "See it Now" profile of McCarthy and his outrageous tactics using McCarthy's own words on March 9, 1954.

Murrow closes the broadcast in his deliberate speaking style: "We will not walk in fear, one of another. We will not be driven by fear into an age of unreason if we dig deep in our history and doctrine and remember that we are not descended from fearful men, not from men who feared to write, to speak, to associate, and to defend causes which were for the moment unpopular. We can deny our heritage and our history, but we cannot escape responsibility for the result. There is no way for a citizen of the Republic to abdicate his responsibility." And later: "Cassius was right. 'The fault, dear Brutus, is not in our stars, but in ourselves.'"

McCarthy is censured by the Senate on December 2, 1954 by sixty-seven senators, and dies of cirrhosis of the liver on May 2, 1957.

BIRTH OF THE "10 MOST WANTED" LIST
March 14, 1950. The F.B.I. inaugurates its "Ten Most Wanted" list. Since then, 484 miscreants have been on the list, and approximately 455 have been captured.

KOREA

June 26, 1950. The Soviet Union misses a vote on the U.N. Security council. The Security Council approves sending ground troops to Korea to prevent troops from North Korea and the People's Republic of China from invading South Korea. (Had they been present, the Soviets would undoubtedly have vetoed it.) The U.N. commits 40,000 troops from fifteen nations. South Korea sends 500,000 troops. The United States commits 300,000 troops. President Harry S. Truman calls this a "police action."

Medal of Honor winner Douglas MacArthur takes command of United Nations troops.

On September 15, 1950, MacArthur directs the troops' landing behind enemy lines at Inchon, one of the largest amphibious assaults in history. China's Chou En-lai warns the U.N. troops to stay south of the Yalu River, the North Korean border with China (then called "Red China"). MacArthur is ordered not to cross the Yalu.

President Truman demands a meeting with MacArthur, and on October 15, 1950, the two meet on Wake Island.

April 11, 1951. General Douglas MacArthur, winner of the Medal of Honor, commander of all United Nations troops in Korea, is relieved of his command by the Commander in Chief, President Harry S. Truman. Although Truman's act is extremely unpopular at the time, Truman confirms civilian control of the Military.

MacArthur dramatically addresses a joint session of Congress on April 19, 1951, and tells them that, after fifty-two years in uniform, in the words of an old song, "Old soldiers never die, they just fade away."

The Korean peace talks drag on interminably. An armistice is signed on May 26, 1953.

FLORENCE CHADWICK

August 8, 1950. Thirty-two-year-old San Diego native Florence Chadwick swims the English Channel from England to France in thirteen hours twenty minutes. She not only breaks Gertrude Ederle's twenty-four-year-old record, but she also becomes the first woman to swim the Channel both ways. Later, she swims from Long Beach to Catalina Island, California, in record time, and swims the Bosphorous, the Strait of Gibraltar, and the Dardanelles.

Chadwick later becomes the swimming instructor at Grossinger's, the legendary all-year resort in New York's Catskill Mountains.

TRUMAN SEIZES THE RAILROADS

August 27, 1950. To prevent a general strike, President Harry Truman seizes the nation's railroads.

THE ATTEMPT TO KILL PRESIDENT TRUMAN

November 1, 1950. The Trumans have temporarily moved out while the White House is undergoing renovations. They are living across the street in Blair House, since 1942 the government's official guest house for visiting dignitaries. While the president takes a nap on the second floor, Oscar Collazo and Griselio Torresola, Puerto Rican nationalists, enter the building and start shooting.

White House police officer Joseph Downs is wounded and Officer Leslie Coffelt shoots and kills Torresola, but not before Coffelt is also shot and killed. Secret Service agent Donald Birdzell is wounded in the leg.

Collazo is arrested, tried, and convicted of felony murder and is sentenced to death. But on July 24, 1952, Harry S. Truman, the man he had tried to assassinate, commutes Collazo's sentence to life in prison—the first time a head of state had commuted the death sentence of a man who had tried to kill him. Collazo spends twenty-nine years in prison before having his life sentence further commuted by President Jimmy Carter.

A LIFETIME CONTRACT! EVEN A-ROD DOESN'T HAVE ONE OF THOSE

1951. Milton Berle, one of the most popular entertainers in the country, known as "Uncle Miltie," and, more importantly, as "Mr. Television," signs a lifetime contract (for thirty years) with N.B.C. for $100,000 per year—a staggering sum at the time. Berle dies in 2002 at the age of ninety-four, having outlived the lifetime contract.

THE UNDEMOCRATIC XXIIND AMENDMENT, LIMITING PRESIDENTIAL TERMS TO TWO, IS RATIFIED

February 27, 1951. The XXIInd Amendment to the Constitution of the United States is ratified. Presidential terms are now limited to two.

F.D.R. haters rejoice!

PLAY BALL! IN COLOR!

AUGUST 11, 1951. C.B.S. BROADCASTS THE FIRST BASEBALL GAME (BROOKLYN DODGERS VS. BOSTON BRAVES FROM BOSTON) IN COLOR.

I WOULDN'T BELIEVE IT IF I HADN'T SEEN IT MYSELF

August 19, 1951. During an otherwise forgettable baseball game at Sportsman's Park in St. Louis between the Browns and the Detroit Tigers, Browns' manager Zach Taylor sends up a pinch hitter who shocks the baseball world and amuses the entire country. The next day, newspapers all across the nation carry a photo of him in the batter's box, even though he draws a walk on four straight pitches.

Why? The pinch hitter is Eddie Gaedel. His plate appearance on this date is his only appearance in a major league game, but it's one of the great moments in baseball history. Eddie Gaedel is three-foot seven-inches tall, wearing uniform #$\frac{1}{8}$—the only fractional uniform number in history. Pitcher Bob "Sugar" Cain can hardly deliver a pitch, he's laughing so hard. Catcher Bob Swift is on his knees.

Browns' owner Bill Veeck stages the event to coincide with the Browns' fiftieth anniversary. Before the game, he tells Gaedel that a sniper will be seated in the bleachers, with a rifle aimed at Gaedel. Veeck warns the midget not to swing the bat upon pain of being shot. After he walks, Gaedel is replaced by pinch runner Jimmy Delsing. Gaedel's baseball career is over. But he remains one of the most famous oddball Veeckian players in history.

THE GIANTS WIN THE PENNANT! THE GIANTS WIN THE PENNANT!

October 3, 1951, 3:58 p.m. The "Shot Heard Round the World" II. In the third game of a three-game play-off, Bobby Thomson of the New York Giants hits a walkoff home run in the bottom of the ninth inning off Brooklyn's Ralph Branca (who wears uniform #13) to win the National League pennant for the Giants. This is one of the most famous (or infamous, if you're a Dodger fan) home runs in history. Also on this date: Future Hall of Famer Dave Winfield is born.

EYE'M WATCHING YOU

OCTOBER 21, 1951. THE C.B.S. "EYE" IS INTRODUCED.

COAST TO COAST ON LIVE T.V.

November 18, 1951. Now that the coaxial has been laid, connecting the nation coast to coast, C.B.S. News airs something never seen before. On Edward R. Murrow's "See it Now," viewers see live video of the Atlantic and Pacific oceans at the same time. It's the first live coast-to-coast commercial broadcast.

PRESIDENT TRUMAN SEIZES THE STEEL MILLS

April 8, 1952. Proclaiming his right to do so as commander in chief in the face of a steelworker's strike, President Harry S. Truman directs the Secretary of Commerce to seize and operate whatever is necessary so that the mills, beset by labor problems, can still make munitions needed for the war in Korea. But on June 2, 1952, the Supreme Court of the United States rules in *Youngstown Sheet & Tube Co. et al. v. Sawyer* that the seizure was unconstitutional.

MR. POTATO HEAD

1952. The first toy to be advertised on television is still going strong. "Mr. Potato Head," invented by George Lerner, contains mostly body parts. Ears, noses, eyes, mouth, glasses, moustache, and later (until he stopped smoking), a pipe. You have to supply your own potato.

THANK YOU, DR. SALK

July 2, 1952. A vaccine against polio is tried for the first time on human beings. Among them are Dr. Jonas Salk, his wife, and children. Dr. Salk developed the vaccine. The vaccine is successful. Polio deaths decline from 28,000 in 1955 to 6,000 in 1957.

In 1962, an oral polio vaccine is developed by Dr. Albert Sabin.

THE MOST TRUSTED MAN IN AMERICA

July 7, 1952. A new word is needed to describe Walter Cronkite's position during the 1952 C.B.S. television broadcasts of the Democratic and Republican national conventions—the first to be televised. The word coined is "anchor." In later years, "Cronkite" becomes a synonym for T.V. news anchor in several languages.

THE CHECKERS SPEECH

September 23, 1952. In the midst of the 1952 campaign, Senator Richard Nixon, the Republican vice presidential candidate, bought time on television. He wanted to refute charges that he had an $18,000 slush fund—money sent for his campaign, which he had diverted for his personal use. He delivers one of his and the nation's most famous (or infamous) speeches.

Sitting at a desk, and then walking around, he tries to tell America that he is honest, and should remain on the ticket. (Eisenhower had been urged to dump Nixon.) Nixon denies the charges one hundred percent. He explained his salary and expenses as a U.S. Senator, a former member of Congress, and a veteran. In a preview of the troubles which forced him to resign as president twenty-two years later, Nixon says: "Because it isn't a question of whether it was legal or illegal, that isn't enough. The question is, was it morally wrong?"

Toward the end of his maudlin, pandering speech, Nixon gets to the subject that gives the speech its name. Someone had sent the Nixons (Richard, his wife Pat, and their daughters Julie and Tricia) a dog.

"It was a little cocker spaniel dog in a crate that he'd sent all the way from Texas. Black and white spotted. And our little girl—Tricia, the six-year-old—named it Checkers. And you know, the kids, like all kids, love the dog and I just want to say this right now, that regardless of what they say about it, we're gonna keep it."

Nixon then dealt with whether he should stay on the ticket with Eisenhower:

"*But the decision, my friends, is not mine. I would do nothing that would harm the possibilities of Dwight Eisenhower to become President of the United States. And for that reason I am submitting to the Republican National Committee tonight through this television broadcast the decision which it is theirs to make.*

Let them decide whether my position on the ticket will help or hurt. And I am going to ask you to help them decide. Wire and write the Republican National Committee whether you think I should stay on or whether I should get off. And whatever their decision is, I will abide by it.

But just let me say this last word. Regardless of what happens I'm going to continue this fight. I'm going to campaign up and down America until we drive the crooks and the Communists and those that defend them out of Washington. And remember, folks, Eisenhower is a great man. Believe me. He's a great man. And a vote for Eisenhower is a vote for what's good for America."

Nixon stayed on the ticket, and on November 4, 1952, Election Day, Eisenhower and Nixon beat Democratic candidates Adlai E. Stevenson (the governor of Illinois) and Senator John Sparkman (U.S. senator from Alabama) by 55.1 percent to 44.4 percent of the popular vote, and 442 electoral votes to the Democrats' 89.

IT'S A BOY!

January 19, 1953. Pregnancy is discussed for the first time on network television. On I Love Lucy, *starring Lucille Ball and Desi Arnaz, "Lucy" gives birth to "Little Ricky." On the same night, Lucille Ball delivers Desi Jr.*

THE ROSENBERGS

June 19, 1953. Julius Rosenberg and his wife Ethel are put to death in the electric chair at Sing Sing prison in Ossining, New York, after their conviction for espionage—giving atomic bomb secrets to the Soviets. Theirs was one of the most infamous trials of the twentieth century—another "crime of the century." To this day, many people believe in their innocence.

BROUGHT TO YOU IN LIVING COLOR

November 22, 1953. The first television program broadcast in color is *The Colgate Comedy Hour* on N.B.C. In an instant, thousands of black and white television sets become obsolete.

HAIL TO THE CHIEF

1954. The Department of Defense (which has jurisdiction over military bands) declares "Hail to the Chief" (a tune dating from 1812) the official music to announce the presence of the president of the United States. The song is preceded by four "ruffles" (drums) and "flourishes" (bugles).

THE FIRST NUCLEAR SHIP

January 21, 1954. The U.S. Navy submarine *Nautilus* (SSN-571), the world's first nuclear-powered submarine, is launched in Groton, Connecticut.

A SHOOTING AT THE CAPITOL

March 1, 1954. Four Puerto Rican nationalists open fire in the House of Representatives, wounding five. They are all arrested, tried, convicted, and sentenced to fifty years in prison.

SEPARATE AND UNEQUAL: *BROWN V. BOARD OF EDUCATION*

May 17, 1954. The Supreme Court of the United States issues its decision in *Brown v. Board of Education of Topeka, Kansas*.

In its unanimous decision, the Court reverses its fifty-eight-year-old "separate but equal" doctrine (*Plessy v. Ferguson*, decided in 1896), and finds that segregated schools violate the 14th Amendment. It orders public schools in the United States desegregated "with all deliberate speed." From this day forward, schools in America must be integrated. But the decision is seen as banning *all* racial segregation. A number of segregated states drag their heels, and are in no rush to comply.

ELVIS

July 5, 1954. A former truck driver from Tupelo, Mississippi, named Elvis Presley makes his first recording, "That's All Right," at Sun Records in Memphis.

THEY ARE BETTER WHEN THEY ARE STALE

1954. Peeps—sugar-drenched marshmallows shaped like chicks, bunnies, pumpkins, or Christmas trees—are introduced. By 2007, over 2,000,000 are produced daily.

WELCOME TO THE JET AGE

July 15, 1954. America enters the jet age—six hours coast to coast—when one of the first Boeing 707 jet planes flies from Renton Field in Washington. The first commercial jet flight is a Pan American World Airways flight on October 26, 1958, from New York to Paris—also about six hours. Jets are faster, smoother, and carry more people than propeller planes.

Few events in history can be said truly to have shrunk the world, i.e., bring people closer together. This is one of them.

The jumbo jet becomes a commercial reality when Pan Am inaugurates its 747 service from New York to London on January 21, 1970. The plane carries 420 passengers. The Wright brothers' first flight could have taken place in the plane's Economy Class cabin.

THE TONIGHT SHOW

September 27, 1954. *The Tonight Show* debuts on N.B.C. The host is the multitalented Steve Allen.

DISNEYLAND OPENS

JULY 17, 1955. DISNEYLAND OPENS IN ANAHEIM, CALIFORNIA—THE FIRST TRULY THEMED AMUSEMENT PARK.

EISENHOWER'S HEART ATTACK

September 24, 1955. President Dwight D. Eisenhower suffers a heart attack while vacationing in Colorado with his wife Mamie's family. Eisenhower recovers at the Fitzsimons Army Medical Center in Denver, wearing pajamas with, variously, five stars, or MUCH BETTER, THANKS, embroidered on them.

THE BROOKLYN DODGERS WIN THE WORLD SERIES FOR THE ONLY TIME

October 4, 1955. "This IS next year!" cry the fans in baseball-crazy Brooklyn, N.Y. The Brooklyn Dodgers—"Dem Bums"—are world champions for the only time in their history, having beaten the New York Yankees in the World Series four games to three. The Dodgers no longer have to complain, "Wait 'Til Next Year."

ROSA PARKS

December 1, 1955. Seamstress Rosa Parks, a black woman, had been working all day and her feet were tired. She boards the local bus in segregated Montgomery, Alabama, and sits in the front. When the bus driver orders her to move to the rear and give up her seat to a white woman, Parks refuses. The driver threatens to have her arrested if she continues to refuse. She refuses again, the police are summoned, and she is arrested. Two-thirds of Montgomery's bus riders at the time are black. By the next day, a boycott of Montgomery's buses by the city's 42,000 blacks is organized by a little-known minister named Martin Luther King Jr. They walk to work, car-pool, and ride bikes. The boycott lasts until a federal court rules the segregated seating is unconstitutional, a ruling upheld by the Supreme Court of the United States. On October 20, 1956, the buses of Montgomery, Alabama, are integrated. Dr. King's philosophy of non-violent protest had been used to make civil rights a national issue, and Dr. King a national figure.

LABOR MERGER

December 5, 1955. The two largest labor organizations in the nation, the Congress of Industrial Organizations and the American Federation of Labor, merge to form a 15 million member organization, the A.F.L.-C.I.O.

LEAR ON WHEELS

January 12, 1956. During a preview of his Broadway production of *King Lear*, Orson Welles breaks his left ankle. On opening night, he plays the role seated in a wheelchair, the shiny wheels obscured by his red robes.

After opening night, he fell backstage and sprained his right ankle.

Welles continued to play Lear from his wheelchair, pushed around the stage by Alvin Epstein, playing the Fool.

THE CORDLESS T.V. REMOTE CONTROLLER

1956. Dr. Robert Adler of Zenith invents the first cordless T.V. remote control.

THE ROLODEX

JANUARY 26, 1956. HILDAUR L. NEILSEN RECEIVES A U.S. PATENT FOR AN ITEM ON THE DESK OF VIRTUALLY EVERY EXECUTIVE AND SECRETARY IN AMERICA: THE ROLODEX CARD FILING SYSTEM.

PERFECT!

October 8, 1956. Don Larsen of the Yankees, a mediocre pitcher by most standards (career: eighty-one wins, ninety-one losses) has a non-mediocre day. Before more than 64,000 fans at Yankee Stadium, Larsen pitches a perfect Game 5 in the World Series, as New York defeat their cross-town rival Brooklyn Dodgers 2–0. The Yankees go on to win the Series 4–3. This is the only post-season perfect game in history.

PLAY-DOH

1956. Play-Doh (available only in off-white) is introduced to the American market by Noah W. McVicker and Joseph S. McVicker.

THE LITTLE ROCK CRISIS: NINE CHILDREN WANT TO GO TO SCHOOL

Fall, 1957. Nine black children try to attend their local high school, Central High School in Little Rock, Arkansas. The students are Elizabeth Eckford, Carlotta Walls, Jefferson Thomas, Thelma Mothershed, Melba Pattillo, Ernest Green, Terrance Roberts, Gloria Ray, and Minnijean Brown. Despite a federal court order, they are refused admission because of their race. The state's governor, Orval Faubus, defies the Supreme Court's ruling in *Brown v. Board of Education*, and calls out the Arkansas National Guard to bar the black students from the school.

On September 14, 1957, President Dwight David Eisenhower meets Gov. Faubus in Newport, Rhode Island (where Eisenhower is vacationing), to discuss the matter. Faubus assures the president that he would allow the black children to enroll. Eisenhower tells him he could continue to keep the National Guard troops at the high school to maintain order. When Faubus returns to Arkansas, he withdraws the Guard troops. Riots break out when the students enter the school to enroll. The governor does not act. Woodrow Mann, the mayor of Little Rock, fearing wider unrest, appeals directly and secretly to Eisenhower on September 23 by telegram, begging him to intervene.

Finally, as a last resort, on September 24, Eisenhower acts. He puts the National Guard troops under federal control—*his* control—and orders the U.S. Army's 101st Airborne Division to Little Rock to restore order and to protect the black students.

On October 4, Eisenhower writes to the parents of the black students: "I believe that America's heart goes out to you and your children in your present ordeal. In the course of our country's progress towards equality of opportunity, you have shown dignity and courage in circumstances which would daunt citizens of lesser faith."

On September 26, Senator Richard Russell, Democrat of Georgia and Chairman of the Senate Armed Services Committee, writes to Eisenhower, and compares the federal troops to "Hitler's storm troopers."

SPUTNIK

October 4, 1957. The first artificial satellite successfully launched into Earth's orbit is *Sputnik*, a sphere about two feet across and weighing about 184 pounds, launched by the Soviet Union.

A second Soviet satellite is launched on November 3, 1957. It carries Laika, the first dog in space. The revelation that the U.S.S.R. is beating the United States in the "space race" is a terrible blow to America's prestige at home and around the world.

The first American satellite in space is *Explorer I*, launched January 31, 1958 to self-congratulatory headlines around the country. *Explorer I* discovers the Van Allen radiation belt. America's joining the U.S.S.R. in space simply adds world-wide excitement to the race to be the first with a man in space. The Soviets win that race, too, when Yuri Gagarin is launched on October 12, 1961 in *Vostok I*, and circles the Earth once in 108 minutes. Americans are distraught that the first man in space is a Soviet (a Russkie!) and not an American.

The day America finally launches a man into space is May 5, 1961, when East Derry, New Hampshire native Lt. Commander Alan B. Shepard of the U.S. Navy is launched for a fifteen-minute suborbital flight. Shepard is feted around the world. He remains in the Navy, and becomes the first astronaut to reach flag rank, retiring as an admiral.

Shepard makes his second trip into space on *Apollo 14*. On February 6, 1971 he pulls out three golf balls and a six iron. Shepard becomes the first man to hit a golf ball on a surface not called "the planet Earth." He leaves one of the balls on the moon. It's still there.

THE FIRST FLIGHT OF THE FRISBEE

1957. The Frisbee (née "Pluto Platter") is introduced.

THE UNKNOWN SOLDIER BECOMES KNOWN

1958. The remains of soldiers buried in Europe, Africa, Hawaii, and the Philippines are exhumed. Two sets of remains—one from the European Theater of Operations and one from the Pacific—are placed in identical caskets and are put aboard the guided missile cruiser U.S.S. *Canberra* off Virginia.

One casket is selected by William R. Charette, the Navy's only serving Medal of Honor recipient. The other casket is buried at sea with honors.

Similarly, the remains of four unknown soldiers from the Korean conflict are disinterred from the National Cemetery of the Pacific in Hawaii. Master Sgt. Ned Lyle makes the selection.

Both caskets lie in state at the U.S. Capitol May 28–30, 1958. They are borne to Arlington on caissons. The president of the United States, and former General of the Army, Dwight D. Eisenhower awards each the Medal of Honor before they are interred in the Tomb of the Unkowns.

When it came time to inter an unknown soldier from the war in Vietnam, identification had become rather sophisticated. There were not many unknowns. And as D.N.A. comparisons became even more precise, almost all remains were identified.

An Unknown Serviceman of the Vietnam Era was selected at Pearl Harbor on May 17, 1984. The selection was made by Marine Corps Sgt. Maj. Allan Jay Kellogg Jr., a recipient of the Medal of Honor. The remains were taken aboard the U.S.S. *Brewton* from Hawaii to Alameda Naval Base in California, then flown to Andrews Air Force Base in Maryland.

On May 28, his remains lay in state at the U.S. Capitol, where President Ronald Reagan visited to pay his respects. They were interred at the Tomb of the Unknowns at Arlington later that day. Mr. Reagan placed a wreath and presented the Medal of Honor. The interment flag was presented to the president as next of kin.

There, the story should have ended. But it didn't. The remains were exhumed on May 14, 1998, because the military decided that the remains were no longer unknown. Mitochondrial D.N.A. testing confirmed that the remains were those of Air Force First Lt. Michael Blassie, shot down near An Loc in 1972.

Lt. Blassie's remains were turned over to his family in St. Louis and Lt. Blassie was buried at the Jefferson Barracks National Cemetery. The crypt at Arlington, which held Lt. Blassie's remains, has been replaced. A sign there now honors America's Missing Servicemen.

THE HULA HOOP

1958. The "Wham-O" company trademarks the name "Hula Hoop" and starts making them out of a petroleum-based product called Marlex. Within six months, they sell 20 million for $1.98 each. A new fad has arrived. If any single product can be considered the embodiment of the late 1950s, it's the Hula Hoop.

FIRST MAJOR LEAGUE GAME ON THE WEST COAST

April 15, 1958. The Los Angeles Dodgers and the San Francisco Giants play the very first major league game on the West Coast, at San Francisco's Seals Stadium, the Giants' temporary home. Giants 8, Dodgers 0. Dodger Gino Cimoli is the first batter. He strikes out.

THE VICUÑA COAT

September 22, 1958. Former New Hampshire Governor Sherman Adams is White House Chief of Staff under President Dwight D. Eisenhower from 1953 to 1958. Adams is forced to resign when it is revealed that he had accepted gifts from Bernard Goldfine, who did business with the federal government. Among the gifts are Oriental rugs and a vicuña coat for Adams's wife. At the time, Goldfine was being investigated by the Federal Trade Commission.

Eisenhower's successor, John F. Kennedy, had no chief of staff. But he was the first former boy scout to be president. Perhaps he was prepared, and didn't need one.

WHAT A GAME!

December 28, 1958. In what many consider the greatest professional football game ever played, the New York Giants play the Baltimore Colts at Yankee Stadium for the championship of the National Football League. The game is tied at seventeen after time runs out, and for the first time, a championship game goes into sudden-death overtime.

The Colts win after an eighty-yard drive on Alan Ameche's one-yard touchdown plunge. Final score: Colts 23, Giants 17. This game, broadcast nationwide on the N.B.C. network, helps make professional football an American passion.

THE DAY THE MUSIC DIED

February 3, 1959. The Beechcraft Bonanza carrying Buddy Holly, J.R. Richardson (The Big Bopper), and Ritchie Valens crashes near Clear Lake, Iowa. All three legends of rock 'n' roll are killed.

RUTH HANDLER: INVENTOR

1959. At the annual Toy Fair in New York City, Ruth Handler introduces a new doll for girls—"Barbie," named for her daughter Barbara. The doll is blonde and has enormous breasts. She's a hit. Since then, over a billion Barbies have been sold. In 1976, Handler—who died of cancer in 2002—invents "Nearly Me," a realistic prosthetic left or right breast in various sizes.

THE 1960 WINTER OLYMPICS IN
SQUAW VALLEY, CALIFORNIA
February 18, 1960. Vice President Richard M. Nixon
opens the VIIIth Winter Olympic Games in Squaw
Valley, California. Because only nine countries are
set to compete, no bobsled run is built—the only
Winter Olympics games without a bobsled
competition. The Gold Medal in men's hockey is
won by the U.S. team.

THE U-2 CRISIS

May 1, 1960. President Dwight D. Eisenhower is going to have a summit meeting on May 16 in Paris with Soviet Premier Nikita Khrushchev. (The fervently anticommunist New York *Daily News* always called Khrushchev "Red Butcher of Hungary.") Prior to the meeting, Eisenhower publicly denies that the United States was sending U-2 spy planes over the U.S.S.R.

This continues to be Eisenhower's position until May 1, 1960, when the Soviets claim to have shot one down with a surface-to-air missile near Svedlovsk and captured the pilot, Francis Gary Powers.

Eisenhower later says that it had been a weather reconnaissance flight, and later still that the C.I.A. had been sending the U-2s, designed to fly at 70,000 feet, thought to be above the capacity of Soviet missiles, without his knowledge or authority.

But Eisenhower refuses Khrushchev's demand for an apology, and "K" cancels the summit.

Powers is tried in Moscow and convicted of espionage. He is sentenced to three years in prison and seven years of hard labor. But he serves only twenty-one months before he is traded on February 10, 1962 on a bridge in Berlin for Soviet spy Rudolph Abel. Powers later becomes a helicopter traffic reporter in Los Angeles, and dies in a helicopter crash on August 1, 1977.

CARYL CHESSMAN EXECUTED

May 2, 1960. Caryl Chessman, a career criminal, is put to death in California's gas chamber. He was identified as the "Red Light Bandit," who impersonated a police officer in order to rob people and sexually abuse women. Although he denies his guilt, Chessman is convicted of kidnapping for profit with bodily harm—not murder, and not rape. Chessman spends twelve years on California's death row, all the while maintaining his innocence. He writes four books while there, including *Cell 2455, Death Row,* which became a best-seller. After eight stays of execution, time runs out, and Chessman is executed.

THE SEXUAL REVOLUTION STARTS NOW

May 9, 1960. Enovid, the first birth-control pill, is approved by the Food and Drug Administration. It was invented by Frank Colton for the G.D. Searle Company. The widespread relatively easy access to "the pill," albeit by prescription only, helps usher in the sexual revolution.

50 STARS IN OUR BANNER

Once Alaska and Hawaii are admitted to the Union in 1959, a new flag is needed. How to design a flag with fifty stars? 10 x 5? 5 x 10? 20 x 2? Robert Heft, a seventeen-year-old high-school junior in Ohio, designs the new flag, alternating lines of five rows of six stars with four rows of five. His design earns him a B in his class, but it is adopted by Congress and becomes official on July 4, 1960. It's been the flag of the United States ever since.

AND UH.......................

August 24, 1960. President Dwight Eisenhower is asked at a press conference to give an example of a major idea of Republican presidential candidate Vice President Richard Nixon that he had adopted as president. Eisenhower's answer: "If you give me a week, I might think of one. I don't remember."

THE KENNEDY–NIXON DEBATE OF 1960

September 28, 1960. Chicago: In a debate unprecedented in American history, both major party presidential candidates hold a televised debate, the first of four. Many who listen to the debate on the radio think that Republican candidate Vice President Richard M. Nixon comes out ahead, but most of those who watch the debate on television believe that Democratic candidate Senator John F. Kennedy of Massachusetts is the winner.

THE NEXT PRESIDENT OF THE UNITED STATES, JOHN F. KENNEDY

November 8, 1960. Senator John Fitzgerald Kennedy is elected President of the United States. At forty-three, he is the youngest man ever elected (Theodore Roosevelt was younger when he succeeded William McKinley upon his death), and is the first president born in the twentieth century. Kennedy is also the first Roman Catholic elected president. Kennedy won the Pulitzer Prize in 1956 while he was a United States senator for *Profiles in Courage*. Kennedy wins the election with 49.7 percent of the popular vote to Vice President Richard M. Nixon's 49.5 percent—a margin of about 100,000 votes. Even though Nixon carries more states than Kennedy, Kennedy wins 303 electoral votes to Nixon's 219.

When the official electoral vote count is announced to the United States Senate, the tally is read by the man who lost: the President of the Senate, Vice President Richard M. Nixon.

HARVEST OF SHAME

November 25, 1960. Edward R. Murrow of C.B.S. News hosts a documentary called *Harvest of Shame* about the plight of America's migrant farm workers. Murrow calls for federal legislation to alleviate their problems.

MR. PRESIDENT! MR. PRESIDENT!
January 25, 1961. John F. Kennedy, president for five days, holds his first formal news conference. It is the first to be broadcast live.

THE XXIIIRD AMENDMENT TO THE CONSTITUTION

March 29, 1961. The XXIIIrd Amendment to the Constitution of the United States is ratified, giving residents of the District of Columbia the right to vote for president. While the District does not have any representation in the Senate, it has a non-voting delegate in the House.

THE BAY OF PIGS

April 15–19, 1961. Just three months after John F. Kennedy became president, the United States assists Cuban exiles in trying to overthrow Fidel Castro's regime. Without significant air support, they are defeated at the "Bay of Pigs." One hundred and four exiles are killed and 1,209 captured in a significant embarrassment for the new president. On December 21, 1962, $53 million in privately raised cash, food, and medicine is paid to ransom 1,113 prisoners.

A VAST WASTELAND

May 9, 1961. Newton Minow, chairman of the Federal Communications Commission—which regulates television—calls television "a vast wasteland." Minow's comment is widely discussed, and many hands are wrung over it. Few disagree with it.

FIRST REVOLVING RESTAURANT IN A CITY

May 22, 1961. The first revolving restaurant in a city is the "Eye of the Needle," atop Seattle's Space Needle.

TO THE MOON!

May 25, 1961. President John F. Kennedy addresses Congress and offers a challenge: "I believe that this nation should commit itself to achieving the goal, before this decade is out, of landing a man on the Moon and returning him safely to the Earth."

Kennedy explains his challenge in a speech at Rice University on September 12, 1962, when he says: "We choose to go to the Moon in this decade and do the other things, not because they are easy, but because they are hard, because that goal will serve to organize and measure the best of our energies and skills, because that challenge is one that we are willing to accept, one we are unwilling to postpone, and one which we intend to win…"

With five months to spare, America does just that: Apollo 11, July 16–24, 1969. While Command Module Pilot Michael Collins orbits the Moon in the command ship *Columbia*, at 4:17:40 p.m. Eastern Daylight Time on July 20 commander Mr. Neil A. Armstrong—Congress had decreed that the first man on the moon must be a civilian—of Wapakoneta, Ohio, and Lunar Module Pilot Air Force Col. Edwin A. "Buzz" Aldrin, of Montclair, New Jersey, land the Lunar Excursion Module *Eagle* on the Sea of Tranquility (0.71 degrees North, 23.63 degrees East, if you are keeping score at home). Armstrong's first words upon setting foot on the lunar surface (July 20,

1969, 10:56:15 p.m. Eastern Daylight Time): "That's one small step for a man, one giant leap for mankind."

The New York *Times* runs three different headlines that day: "MEN LAND ON MOON"; followed by "MAN WALKS ON MOON"; and finally "MEN WALK ON MOON."

Armstrong and Aldrin collected 21.7 kilograms of rocks, planted the American flag (no U.N. flag, by act of Congress), and implanted a commemorative plaque ("HERE MEN FROM THE PLANET EARTH FIRST SET FOOT UPON THE MOON, JULY, 1969 A.D. WE CAME IN PEACE FOR ALL MANKIND"), complete with Richard M. Nixon's signature.[1] They were on the lunar surface for a total of 21 hours and 38 minutes and 21 seconds.

Upon their return to Earth, Nixon throws a party for the three astronauts at Century Plaza in Los Angeles. The only members of minority groups to attend were members of the diplomatic corps and actor Caesar Romero.

---

[1] I am still waiting for the next lunar mission to take Nixon's name *off* my Moon.

SUPPRESSION MOTIONS

June 19, 1961. The Supreme Court of the United States decides *Mapp v. Ohio*. The Court holds that evidence seized through an illegal search and seizure may not be offered at trial. This is a monumental ruling in the field of criminal law. The "exclusionary rule" is still roundly criticized today.

SIX CRISES

1962. Richard M. Nixon's autobiography, *Six Crises*, is published. It includes chapters on, among other things, the Alger Hiss case, President Eisenhower's heart attack, and Nixon's loss to John F. Kennedy in 1960. That chapter is called "Defeat." By the time the book is reprinted, Nixon is considering a run for the presidency in 1968. The chapter about the 1960 election is retitled "The Campaign of 1960."

A TOUR OF THE WHITE HOUSE

February 14, 1962. First Lady Jacqueline Kennedy gives C.B.S. correspondent Charles Collingwood a tour of the White House. Because it was re-broadcast in over fifty countries, this becomes the most-viewed documentary of all time.

GODSPEED, JOHN GLENN

February 20, 1962. John Glenn becomes the first American to orbit the Earth, as he travels three orbits in four hours, fifty-five minutes. His Mercury capsule is named *Friendship Seven*. During the Korean War, Glenn was a Marine wing commander. One of the fliers under his command was Ted Williams. Glenn is lauded as a true American hero. He goes on to serve as a Democratic United States senator from Ohio, 1974–1999.

On October 29, 1988, Glenn returns to space for eight days and twenty-one hours as a payload specialist on the Space Shuttle *Discovery*. His mission: to determine the effects of space travel on a seventy-seven-year-old man.

ONE PERSON, ONE VOTE

March 26, 1962. The Supreme Court of the United States decides *Baker v. Carr*, requiring that state legislatures be apportioned on the basis of population—"one man, one vote." Earl Warren, who was Chief Justice from 1953 through 1969, and who presided over many decisions that expanded the rights of ordinary Americans, often said that he was most proud of this decision, for it provided to millions the right to vote and to have their vote counted fairly.

JAMES MEREDITH

September 10, 1962. The Supreme Court of the United States, in a suit brought by the N.A.A.C.P. Legal Defense and Educational Fund, Inc., orders the University of Mississippi to admit James Meredith, a black student at Jackson State College, an all-black school. There had never been a black student at Ole Miss. Ross Barnett, the state's racist governor, did everything he could to block Meredith's admission, including standing in the schoolhouse door.

With the help of U.S. Attorney General Robert F. Kennedy, U.S. Marshals, Border Patrol agents, and even federal prison guards, a deal is struck with Barnett. Meredith will be allowed to register. He is met by a mob of 2,000 angry protesters who throw Molotov cocktails, bricks, and bottles. The riot takes two lives. Twenty-eight U.S. Marshals are shot and 160 injured. (In the "Hospitality State"!)

On October 1, Meredith registers. He completes his college education and is graduated in 1964.

HEEEEEEEERE'S JOHNNY!

October 1 1962. Thirty-seven-year-old Johnny Carson debuts as the host of N.B.C.'s *The Tonight Show* from New York. He becomes the most popular and influential late-night TV host ever. For young comedians, singers, impressionists, magicians, and other entertainers, an appearance on *The Tonight Show* is a career-maker.

THE CUBAN MISSILE CRISIS

October 15, 1962. Soviet SS-4 missiles are discovered in Cuba by an American U-2 spy plane, piloted by Richard Heyser.

October 16, 1962. President John F. Kennedy is informed about the Cuban missiles.

October 17–19, 1962. President Kennedy informs Soviet Foreign Minister Andrie Gromyko that the United States will not tolerate Soviet missiles in Cuba. According to Gromyko, there are no Soviet missiles in Cuba. Gromyko does not know that Kennedy has seen the photos. But Kennedy knows that Gromyko is lying.

October 22, 1962. In a televised address to the nation, Kennedy announces that U.S. intelligence has discovered Soviet offensive missiles in Cuba, just ninety miles from Florida. He demands that Soviet leader Nikita S. Krushchev remove them. Meanwhile, he orders a quarantine—actually a blockade—of Cuba, to be enforced by the U.S. Navy. For seven days the two nuclear superpowers are on the brink of war.

October 25, 1962. America's United Nations Ambassador Adlai E. Stevenson demands an answer from the Soviet ambassador, Valerian Zorin, regarding the missiles. When Zorin tells Stevenson that he will have his answer "in due course," Stevenson replies: "I am prepared to wait for my answer until hell freezes over."

October 28, 1962. Krushchev concedes and agrees to remove the missiles.

THE MURDER OF MEDGAR EVERS

June 12, 1963. Medgar Evers, field secretary for the Mississippi N.A.A.C.P. is shot and killed in his driveway. Byron De La Beckwith is tried twice for the crime in state court, but no verdict is reached in either trial. In 1993, he is tried again, convicted, and sentenced to life imprisonment.

SCHOOL PRAYERS, YES. FORCED SCHOOL PRAYERS, NO.
April 3, 1962. The Supreme Court of the United States decides Engel v. Vitale*, barring* forced *prayer in public schools.*

SIX HONORARY CITIZENS OF THE UNITED STATES

April 9, 1963. The highest honor the United States can bestow on a foreigner is making him or her an honorary citizen of the United States by act of Congress. This singular honor has been granted only six times, and only twice to living people:

Winston S. Churchill, Prime Minister of England, and leader of his country during its darkest days, World War II. Honorary American citizenship conferred April 9, 1963.

Marie Joseph Paul Yves Roche Gilbert du Motier, the Marquis de Lafayette of France, who helped train troops for George Washington. Honorary American citizenship conferred August 6, 2002.

Agnes Gonxha Bojaxhiu, better known as Mother Teresa of Calcutta. Honorary American citizenship conferred October 1, 1996. The Macedonian-born Missionaries of Charity nun, of

Albanian ancestry, was awarded the Nobel Peace Prize in 1985, and was beatified in 2003.

William Penn, British-born governor of Pennsylvania, and his second wife, Hannah Callowhill Penn, administrator of the Province of Pennsylvania for six years. Honorary American citizenship conferred on both, November 28, 1984.

Raoul Wallenberg of Sweden. The First Secretary at the Swedish embassy in Budapest during World War II, Wallenberg saved thousands of Hungarian Jews by granting them documents conferring Swedish citizenship. Honorary American citizenship conferred October 5, 1981. Wallenberg was also made an honorary citizen of Canada. He and Nelson Mandela are the only two people to have received that honor.

GIDEON

March 18, 1963. The Supreme Court of the United States unanimously decides the landmark case of *Gideon v. Wainright*, holding that every person charged with a crime—not just in death penalty cases—is entitled to a lawyer. If the accused cannot afford a lawyer, the government must provide one free of charge.

THE MARCH ON WASHINGTON

August 28, 1963. The March on Washington. The Rev. Dr. Martin Luther King Jr. delivers his "I have a dream" speech from the steps of the Lincoln Memorial, before a crowd estimated at 250,000—one of the most influential and stirring speeches in American history:

"I am happy to join with you today in what will go down in history as the greatest demonstration for freedom in the history of our nation. Five score years ago, a great American, in whose symbolic shadow we stand today, signed the Emancipation Proclamation. This momentous decree came as a great beacon light of hope to millions of Negro slaves who had been seared in the flames of withering injustice. It came as a joyous daybreak to end the long night of their captivity.

But one hundred years later, the Negro still is not free. One hundred years later, the life of the Negro is still sadly crippled by the manacles of segregation and the chains of discrimination. One hundred years later, the Negro lives on a lonely island of poverty in the midst of a vast ocean of material prosperity. One hundred years later, the Negro is still languishing in the corners of American society and finds himself an exile in his own land. So we have come here today to dramatize a shameful condition.

In a sense we have come to our nation's capital to cash a check. When the architects of our republic wrote the magnificent words of the Constitution and the Declaration of Independence, *they were signing a promissory note to which every American was to fall heir. This note was a promise that all men, yes, black men as well as white men, would be guaranteed the unalienable rights of life, liberty, and the pursuit of happiness.*

It is obvious today that America has defaulted on this promissory note insofar as her citizens of color are concerned. Instead of honoring this sacred obligation, America has given the Negro people a bad check, a check which has come back marked 'insufficient funds.' But we refuse to believe that the bank of justice is bankrupt. We refuse to believe that there are insufficient funds in the great vaults of opportunity of this nation. So we have come to cash this check—a check that will give us upon demand the riches of freedom and the security of justice. We have also come to this hallowed spot to remind America of the fierce urgency of now. This is no time to engage in the luxury of cooling off or to take the tranquilizing drug of gradualism. Now is the time to make real the promises of democracy. Now is the time to rise from the dark and desolate valley of segregation to the sunlit path of racial justice. Now is the time to lift our nation from the quick sands of racial injustice to the solid rock of brotherhood. Now is the time to make justice a reality for all of God's children.

It would be fatal for the nation to overlook the urgency of the moment. This sweltering summer of the Negro's legitimate discontent will not pass until there is an invigorating autumn of freedom and equality. Nineteen sixty-three is not an end, but a beginning. Those who hope that the Negro needed to blow off steam and will now be content will have a rude awakening if the nation returns to business as usual. There will be neither rest nor tranquility in America until the Negro is granted his citizenship rights. The whirlwinds of revolt will continue to shake the foundations of our nation until the bright day of justice emerges.

But there is something that I must say to my people who stand on the warm threshold which leads into the palace of justice. In the process of gaining our rightful place we must not be guilty of wrongful deeds. Let us not seek to satisfy our thirst for freedom by drinking from the cup of bitterness and hatred.

We must forever conduct our struggle on the high plane of dignity and discipline. We must not allow our creative protest to degenerate into physical violence. Again and again we must rise to the majestic heights of meeting physical force with soul force. The marvelous new militancy which has engulfed the Negro community must not lead us to distrust of all white people, for many of our white brothers, as evidenced by their presence here today, have come to realize that their destiny is tied up with our destiny and their freedom is inextricably bound to our freedom. We cannot walk alone.

As we walk, we must make the pledge that we shall march ahead. We cannot turn back. There are those who are asking the devotees of civil rights, 'When will you be satisfied?' We can never be satisfied as long as the Negro is the victim of the unspeakable horrors of police brutality. We can never be satisfied, as long as our bodies, heavy with the fatigue of travel, cannot gain lodging in the motels of the highways and the hotels of the cities. We can never be satisfied as long as a Negro in Mississippi cannot vote and a Negro in New York believes he has nothing for which to vote. No, no, we are not satisfied, and we will not be satisfied until justice rolls down like waters and righteousness like a mighty stream.

I am not unmindful that some of you have come here out of great trials and tribulations. Some of you have come fresh from narrow jail cells. Some of you have come from areas where your quest for freedom left you battered by the storms of persecution and staggered by the winds of police brutality. You have been the veterans of creative suffering. Continue to work with the faith that unearned suffering is redemptive.

Go back to Mississippi, go back to Alabama, go back to South Carolina, go back to Georgia, go back to Louisiana, go back to the slums and ghettos of our northern cities, knowing that somehow this situation can and will be changed. Let us not wallow in the valley of despair.

I say to you today, my friends, so even though we face the difficulties of today and tomorrow, I still have a dream. It is a dream deeply rooted in the American dream.

I have a dream that one day this nation will rise up and live out the true meaning of its creed: 'We hold these truths to be self-evident: that all men are created equal.'

I have a dream that one day on the red hills of Georgia the

sons of former slaves and the sons of former slave owners will be able to sit down together at the table of brotherhood.

I have a dream that one day even the state of Mississippi, a state sweltering with the heat of injustice, sweltering with the heat of oppression, will be transformed into an oasis of freedom and justice.

I have a dream that my four little children will one day live in a nation where they will not be judged by the color of their skin but by the content of their character.

I have a dream today.

I have a dream that one day, down in Alabama, with its vicious racists, with its governor having his lips dripping with the words of interposition and nullification; one day right there in Alabama, little black boys and black girls will be able to join hands with little white boys and white girls as sisters and brothers.

I have a dream today.

I have a dream that one day every valley shall be exalted, every hill and mountain shall be made low, the rough places will be made plain, and the crooked places will be made straight, and the glory of the Lord shall be revealed, and all flesh shall see it together.

This is our hope. This is the faith that I go back to the South with. With this faith we will be able to hew out of the mountain of despair a stone of hope. With this faith we will be able to transform the jangling discords of our nation into a beautiful symphony of brotherhood. With this faith we will be able to work together, to pray together, to struggle together, to go to jail together, to stand up for freedom together, knowing that we will be free one day.

This will be the day when all of God's children will be able to sing with a new meaning, 'My country, 'tis of thee, sweet land of liberty, of thee I sing. Land where my fathers died, land of the pilgrim's pride, from every mountainside, let freedom ring.'

And if America is to be a great nation this must become true. So let freedom ring from the prodigious hilltops of New Hampshire. Let freedom ring from the mighty mountains of New York. Let freedom ring from the heightening Alleghenies of Pennsylvania!

Let freedom ring from the snowcapped Rockies of Colorado!

Let freedom ring from the curvaceous slopes of California!

But not only that; let freedom ring from Stone Mountain of Georgia!

Let freedom ring from Lookout Mountain of Tennessee!

Let freedom ring from every hill and molehill of Mississippi. From every mountainside, let freedom ring.

And when this happens, when we allow freedom to ring, when we let it ring from every village and every hamlet, from every state and every city, we will be able to speed up that day when all of God's children, black men and white men, Jews and Gentiles, Protestants and Catholics, will be able to join hands and sing in the words of the old Negro spiritual, 'Free at last! free at last! thank God Almighty, we are free at last!'"

THE NETWORKS' EVENING NEWSCASTS EXPAND TO THIRTY MINUTES

September 3, 1963. "The C.B.S. Evening News with Walter Cronkite" expands from fifteen to thirty minutes, the first network news program to do so.

PRESIDENT JOHN F. KENNEDY ASSASSINATED

November 22, 1963. John Fitzgerald Kennedy, the thirty-fifth President of the United States, is shot and killed in Dallas, Texas, by a lone gunman named Lee Harvey Oswald. Later that day, Vice President Lyndon Baines Johnson is sworn in as president by United States Magistrate Sarah T. Hughes on Air Force One at Love Field, Dallas's airport, flanked by Mrs. Johnson and Mrs. Kennedy.

Oswald was himself murdered in the basement of Dallas Police Headquarters on November 24, 1963 by strip-club owner Jack Ruby.

When asked for his comment on Oswald's murder, Richard M. Nixon, arriving in Washington for Kennedy's funeral, stammers: "I have always said that two rights do not make a wr—I mean, two wrongs do not make a right."

THE WARREN COMMISSION

November 29, 1963. Less than a week after President Kennedy's assassination, President Lyndon B. Johnson appoints a commission to investigate the assassination. He asks (more like a command when Lyndon Johnson did the asking) Earl Warren, the respected Chief Justice of the United States, to be the chairman. Warren reluctantly accepts.

On September 24, 1964, the Commission presents its findings to President Johnson, and in October 1964, the 912-page report is released to the nation. The Commission's conclusion, which is roundly criticized, finds that Lee Harvey Oswald and nobody else was responsible for John F. Kennedy's murder.

Operators who answered the Warren Commission's phones found it too cumbersome to say, "Commission to Investigate the Assassination of President John F. Kennedy, good morning." So they just answered the phone, "Assassination."

LET'S GO TO THE VIDEOTAPE

December 7, 1963. The C.B.S. broadcast of the annual Army–Navy football game is the first to use "Instant Replay."

ED SULLIVAN, ED SULLIVAN, WE'RE GOING TO BE ON ED SULLIVAN

February 9, 1964. The Beatles appear on Ed Sullivan's T.V. show for the first time. They are paid $10,000 plus expenses. They sing "All My Loving," "Till There Was You" (from "The Music Man"!), "She Loves You," "I Saw Her Standing There," and "I Want To Hold Your Hand." Some 73 million Americans watch. The Beatles' four appearances on Sullivan's show that year (this one plus February 16, February 23, and May 24) are watched by over 250 million viewers, an average of 63.3 million per appearance. The "British Invasion" of rock 'n' roll singers and musicians is on.

KITTY GENOVESE

March 13, 1964, 3:20 a.m. Twenty-eight-year-old Catherine "Kitty" Genovese is stabbed to death outside her home in Kew Gardens, Queens, New York. Thirty-eight of her neighbors hear her agonized cries for help and do nothing. They don't want to get involved.

Winston Mosley is arrested for the gruesome crime, charged, tried, and convicted. Mosley is sentenced to death, but the sentence is later reduced to life in prison.

The Kitty Genovese case is often cited as an example of urban alienation and is the embodiment, perhaps, of the "I don't want to get involved" mentality.

GOODMAN, CHANEY, AND SCHWERNER

June 21, 1964. Andrew Goodman, James Chaney, and Michael Schwerner, three young civil rights workers, are murdered near Philadelphia, Mississippi. Their killers, including the local sheriff, are arrested, tried, and convicted under the new federal civil rights laws.

RALPH NADER

1965. Ralph Nader, a Harvard Law School graduate, publishes his first book, *Unsafe at Any Speed*. The book is an attack on the newest car from General Motors, the Chevrolet "Corvair." Nader testifies before a Senate committee, and his charges against G.M. really sting. So much so that General Motors hires private detectives to see what they can "find" on Nader's private life. Nader sues. He collects $280,000. General Motors apologizes. But the subject of automotive safety jumps to the forefront on the national agenda. Seatbelts, airbags, more stability in chassis frames—all directly attributable to this one private citizen who never held public office[2]. Nader creates public interest law firms to make or to keep large corporations and industries honest and to look out for the consumer. The consumer protection industry can be said to start with Ralph Nader and his "Nader's Raiders."

[2] Not for lack of trying. Nader was the presidential candidate of the Green Party in 2002. He siphoned off enough votes, which probably would have gone to Al Gore, to help George W. Bush take the White House.

MALCOLM X

February 21, 1965. Malcolm X—the charismatic black leader— is shot and killed in New York City. He is thirty-nine.

He was born Malcolm Little in Omaha, Nebraska. His father was murdered and his mother wound up in a mental hospital. Little became a cocaine addict and was sentenced to ten years in prison for burglary. While in prison, he converted to the Black Muslim faith. He met Nation of Islam leader Elijah Muhammad (Poole) and changed his name to Malcolm X, rejecting Little as a slave name. In New York, he was the founder and editor of *Muhammad Speaks*, the Nation of Islam newspaper, and he was a regular speaker for the Nation of Islam. He established a number of mosques in New York. Unlike other black leaders, Malcolm X rejected integration. He preached black power instead of racial equality. His views on racial coexistence became more extreme, and Elijah Muhammad suspended him. When President John F. Kennedy was assassinated, he said that the "chickens had come home to roost."

Malcolm separated from the Nation of Islam in 1964 and formed his own sect, the Organization of Afro-American Unity. But after a pilgrimage to Mecca, his views evolved. Now, he was in favor of world brotherhood.

On February 21, 1965, he was shot to death at the Audubon Ballroom in Harlem, New York City. Three Black Muslims were convicted of the crime.

THE VOTING RIGHTS ACT OF 1965

March 7, 1965. Six hundred peaceful civil rights protesters march along U.S. Route 80 from Selma, Alabama, on their way to the state capital in Montgomery, to demand the right to vote and an end to racial segregation. They try to cross the Edmund Pettus Bridge in Selma. They are attacked by law enforcement officers with night sticks and tear gas.

Two days later, the Rev. Dr. Martin Luther King Jr. visits the bridge, and seeks a court order to permit the march. The judge who had desegregated the public buses in Montgomery after the Rosa Parks-inspired boycott, U.S. District Court Judge Frank M. Johnson, Jr.—a true hero in American history—permits the march and notes: "The law is clear that the right to petition one's government for the redress of grievances may be exercised in large groups...and these rights may be exercised by marching, even along public highways."

By March 21, the protest has been reorganized. Some 3,200 protesters are back, walking twelve miles a day towards Montgomery. About 25,000 join the protest at the state capitol.

On August 6, 1965, President Lyndon Baines Johnson of Texas signs the historic Voting Rights Act of 1965. Literacy tests for voting are prohibited. No new restrictions on voting can be implemented in certain areas of the country with a history of segregation and racial discrimination—i.e., the Southern states—unless the Attorney General of the United States, or the Federal Court in Washington, decide that the new rule would not lead to further segregation or discrimination. Federal observers and federal examiners help enforce the new law.

In 1996, the *Selma to Montgomery National Historic Trail* is established by act of Congress. It is now considered an "All-American Road" of national historic significance. The route is itself a destination.

THE DAY THAT THE POPE CAME TO NEW YORK

October 4, 1965. Pope Paul VI celebrates the first papal mass in North America at Yankee Stadium in New York before 80,000 people—the "Sermon on the Mound." Paul is the first pope to visit America. He comes to plead for world peace at the United Nations. After he left, the joke was told that the pope had to return to Yankee Stadium—he forgot to touch second base.

THE FIRST BLACK MAJOR LEAGUE UMPIRE

April 11, 1966. Emmett Ashford becomes the first black man to umpire a major league game, Cleveland Indians vs. Washington Senators. Upon his death on March 1, 1980, Ashford is buried in Cooperstown, New York.

WHAT IS THIS STUFF? NOT GRASS

April 18, 1966. The Houston Astros and the visiting Los Angeles Dodgers play the first game ever on a surface other than grass. "Astroturf" is used for Opening Day at the Harris County Domed Stadium—the Houston Astrodome, the first domed stadium, dubbed "The Eighth Wonder of the World."

YOU HAVE THE RIGHT TO REMAIN SILENT

June 13, 1966. The Supreme Court of the United States decides the landmark case of *Miranda v. Arizona*. Before a custodial interrogation may begin, police will now be required to inform the suspect that 1. You have the right to remain silent. 2. Anything you say may be used against you in a court of law. 3. You have the right to have an attorney present. 4. If you cannot afford an attorney, one will be provided to you free of charge. After the decision, many police officers carry the "Miranda warnings" on a card in their hats.

And a new word enters the language: "Mirandize." "Charlie, you just arrested this suspect. Did you Mirandize her yet?"

While law enforcement officers loudly complain for years that the Supreme Court is "handcuffing the police" with this new policy, British police have been giving their suspects similar warnings for years. Inspector Lestrade of Scotland Yard tells Mr. Sherlock Holmes frequently that someone he had arrested had been "cautioned"—given what amounted to his Miranda rights

N.O.W.

JUNE 30, 1966. THE NATIONAL ORGANIZATION FOR WOMEN IS FOUNDED.

BORN TO RAISE HELL

July 10, 1966. Richard Speck, a drifter, kills eight student nurses in Chicago. It is one of America's worst and most revolting mass killings. Speck is later identified because of his truthful tattoo: "BORN TO RAISE HELL." Speck's death sentence is later reduced to life in prison, but after only nineteen years in prison Speck dies of a heart attack on December 5, 1991. His body is unclaimed.

TUNE IN, TURN ON, DROP OUT, BUT ONLY UNTIL OCTOBER 5

October 5, 1966. The last day on which Lysergic acid diethylamide is legal in the State of California. The sale, possession, and manufacture of L.S.D. becomes illegal in California the next day. But bananas are still legal, and many people try to get high on baked banana skins. It does not work.

KWANZAA

December 26, 1966. The first celebration of Kwanzaa, invented by Dr. Maulana Karenga, an African-American holiday designed to celebrate unity, self-determination, cooperation, support, community ties, creativity, and faith.

SUPER BOWL I

January 15, 1967. The first "Super Bowl" is played. Oops. Make that Super Bowl I. It pits the Green Bay Packers of the National Football League against the Kansas City Chiefs of the upstart American Football League. Green Bay 35, K.C. 10. Super Bowl II, January 14, 1968, is another victory for the Packers: Green Bay 33, Oakland 14—reaffirming the dominance of the staid, old N.F.L. But Super Bowl III is quite different. It features the N.F.L.'s Baltimore Colts against the Joe Namath-led New York Jets of the A.F.L. Namath guarantees a Jet victory. And he delivers: Jets 16, Colts 7.

The victory gives the young A.F.L. parity with the N.F.L., and leads ultimately to their merger. Super Bowl III also helps establish professional football as a national obsession and "Broadway" Joe Namath as one of its superstars.

APOLLO I

January 27, 1967. A still unexplained flash fire in the command module of Apollo I during a launch pad test takes the lives of astronauts Edward White, Roger Chaffee, and Virgil I. "Gus" Grissom, America's second man in space. The Command Module is redesigned after the fire.

ALI, ALI

April 28, 1967. Cassius Marcellus Clay, "The Louisville Lip," wins the gold medal as a light heavyweight boxer in the 1960 Olympics in Rome. After he turns professional, he beats Sonny Liston on February 25, 1964 in Miami Beach to become the heavyweight champion of the world. He later converts to Islam, changes his name to Muhammad Ali, and becomes a Muslim minister. He is drafted into the U.S. Army. On April 28, 1967, at the Army induction center in Houston, he refuses to take the one step forward required for induction, proclaiming his status as a minister of the Muslim faith. Says Ali: "I ain't got no quarrel with them Viet Cong." Ali is charged with draft evasion, convicted, and sentenced to five years in prison.

The day of his refusal, the New York State Athletic Commission and the World Boxing Association revoke Ali's license to fight and declares the championship open. He is without a job.

But Ali believes that a title which he won in the ring can only be lost in the ring, not by fiat of the State Athletic Commission.

Ali challenges the Commission's decision in court. His lawyer, Michael Meltsner, provides the court with a list of ninety fighters who had been granted licenses despite felony convictions for such crimes as murder, burglary, and rape. Another fifteen had been granted licenses despite military crimes such as desertion and assault. On September 14, 1970, a federal judge rules that the Commission had been arbitrary and unreasonable in denying Ali a license, and orders his license restored. It had taken Ali three years—three of his *prime* years—to regain his license to fight. (His conviction for draft evasion is overturned by the Supreme Court of the United States by a vote of 8–0 on June 28, 1971.)

Not having fought in three years, Ali has to reestablish himself in the ring. So he takes on Jerry Quarry and Oscar Bonavena and beats them both.

Then he fights for the title—*his* title—at New York's Madison Square Garden in one of the most anticipated, exciting, talked-about prizefights of all time. On March 8, 1971, Ali fights the current heavyweight champion, twenty-seven-year-old "Smokin'" Joe Frazier (26–0 with 23 knockouts). Frazier weighs 203 pounds. Ali, twenty-nine years old, weighs 215 pounds for the fight. He is three inches taller than Frazier. Ali is undefeated (31–0 with 25 knockouts).

The purse is a record 2.5 million dollars. Tickets are $150—if you can get one, and you can't. 20,455 fans pack the Garden. Some 300 million watch on closed-circuit TV[3]. Burt Lancaster calls the fight on the radio. This is the fight of the century—two undefeated heavyweight champions, fighting for the title.

Seven hundred reporters have credentials for the fight. One of them is *Life* magazine's special photographer Frank Sinatra.

The fight lasts until 2:34 of the fifteenth and final round. Ali goes down. All three judges give the fight to Frazier. Ali has lost for the first time in his career.

Ali and Frazier fight again—a non-title fight in 1974 (which Ali wins) and again in 1975, when Ali regains the World Heavyweight title. But the first fight was one of the monumental fights of the century, because of the out-of-the-ring history leading up to it.

On September 15, 2000, Muhammad Ali is named a Messenger of Peace by United Nations Secretary General Kofi Annan.

On November 9, 2005, President George W. Bush gives Ali the Medal of Freedom, the nation's highest civilian honor.

[3] Author's note: That's how I saw it.

BANS ON INTERRACIAL MARRIAGE BANNED

June 12, 1967. The Supreme Court of the United States announces its decision in *Loving v. Virginia*, unanimously finding anti-miscegenation (also known as interracial marriage) laws unconstitutional.

MR. JUSTICE THURGOOD MARSHALL

June 13, 1967. Thurgood Marshall is appointed to the Supreme Court of the United States by President Lyndon B. Johnson. Marshall is the first black named to the High Court. Marshall serves until 1991.

HAIR

October 17, 1967. "Hair" opens off-Broadway and moves to Broadway April 29, 1968. The "American Tribal Love-Rock Musical" is a big hit. "Hair" runs for 1,873 performances. One scene includes both men and women on stage, totally nude. When *New York Post* columnist Leonard Lyons asked his wife Sylvia what she thought of the show, with naked men and women, she replied, "There were naked women?"

L.B.J.'S GOING AWAY

March 31, 1968. After four and a half years in office, and increasingly loud anti-war demonstrations and sentiment throughout the country, President Lyndon Baines Johnson makes a surprise announcement during a televised nation-wide address from the Oval Office: "I will not seek, nor will I accept, the nomination of my party for another term as your president." Johnson thought that if he devoted the rest of his term to bringing peace to Vietnam, he would hasten an end to the war. During the last months of his presidency, the only places he can make a speech without fear of hecklers ("Hey, hey, L.B.J.! How many kids did you kill today?") or picketers is on military bases.

THE REV. DR. MARTIN LUTHER KING JR. MURDERED

April 4, 1968. The Rev. Dr. Martin Luther King Jr., standing on a balcony at the Lorraine Motel in Memphis, Tennessee, where he had come to encourage striking sanitation workers, is shot and killed by James Earl Ray. Dr. King was the most charismatic orator of the civil rights movement and was the winner of the 1964 Nobel Peace Prize—at thirty-five, the youngest man to be so honored.

THE GATEWAY ARCH

May 25, 1968. The Gateway Arch, saluting the Lewis and Clark expedition and America's westward expansion, is dedicated in St. Louis, Missouri. At 630 feet tall, the monument, designed by Eero Saarinen, is the nation's tallest.

ANDY WARHOL SHOT

June 3, 1968, 4:20 p.m. Artist Andy Warhol, thirty-nine, one of America's most popular artists, and the king of Pop Art as well as the creator of many off-beat films, is shot and seriously wounded in the side and abdomen while in his film studio. At the time of the shooting, Warhol is speaking on the phone with Viva, who appeared in a number of his films. Warhol was in surgery for four hours.

The assailant is Valerie Solanas, twenty-eight, who has appeared in one of his films. She says that he is a member of the previously unknown S.C.U.M., the Society for Cutting up Men. Solanas claims that Warhol had too much control over her life.

Warhol makes a full recovery.

Solanas enters a plea of guilty after Warhol refuses to testify against her. Solanas is sentenced to three years in prison.

The Warhol shooting would have dominated the headlines for weeks, but it is reduced to eight-point type on page ninety-three of most newspapers three days later, when Robert Kennedy is assassinated.

ROBERT F. KENNEDY ASSASSINATED

June 5, 1968. Robert Francis Kennedy, the junior senator from New York, a former Attorney General of the United States, the younger brother of President John F. Kennedy and Senator Ted Kennedy, and a candidate for the Democratic nomination for president, is shot and killed by Sirhan Sirhan in the kitchen of the Ambassador Hotel in Los Angeles on the night Kennedy wins California's presidential primary. His last public words: "And now, on to Chicago!" [where the Democratic convention was to be held].

THE LOOOOOOOOOOOOOOOOOOOOOOONG JUMP

October 15, 1968. American Bob Beamon wins the long jump at the Olympics in Mexico City, with a mark of 29' 2^1/$_2$". He breaks the previous world long jump record, set by Jesse Owens at the 1936 Berlin Olympics, by 21^3/$_4$".

FOUR FOR OERTER

October 15, 1968. Al Oerter wins at the Mexico City Olympics—his fourth consecutive Olympic gold medal in the discus—and beats his personal best by *five feet*.

THE BLACK POWER SALUTE AT THE OLYMPICS

October 17, 1968. After winning the gold and bronze medals, respectively, in the 200 meters at the Olympic Games in Mexico City, Americans Tommy Smith and John Carlos stand on the medal platform (along with Silver medalist Peter Norman of Australia). They make a statement about the status of African-Americans in the United States and the world, but they do so without uttering a word. Smith and Carlos are shoeless—to symbolize the plight of poor blacks in America—and they wear beads, to symbolize the blacks murdered or lynched in the U.S. Finally, Carlos and Smith close their eyes, bow their heads, and hold up gloved fists as the "Star-Spangled Banner" is played (Smith on his right hand, Carlos on his left). The gloved fists are meant to symbolize the unity of black Americans in opposition to racism and oppression. Smith said the protest was a symbol of Black Power in America.

Smith and Carlos pay a heavy price for their silent, dignified protest: They are kicked off the relay teams, thrown out of the Olympic Village, and sent home.

Their provocative protest, seen by tens of millions on television, sends a powerful message around the world—a symbol of Black Power and black freedom.

"IN THE BEGINNING…"

December 21–27, 1968. American astronauts Frank Borman, Jim Lovell, and Bill Anders pilot Apollo 8 *to orbit the Moon, the first Earthlings to do so. When they circle behind the Moon, they are farther away from Earth than any people have ever been—truly, into the unknown. They broadcast back to Earth from lunar orbit on Christmas Eve, reading the story of creation from the Bible. Anders reads from Genesis 1:1–4. "In the beginning God created the heaven and the earth. And the earth was without form, and void; and darkness was upon the face of the deep. And the Spirit of God moved upon the face of the waters. And God said, 'Let there be light': and there was light. And God saw the light, that it was good: and God divided the light from the darkness." Subsequent verses were read by Lovell and Borman.*

THE ONLY PRIME-TIME T.V. SHOW WITHOUT MUSIC
SEPTEMBER 24, 1968. "60 MINUTES" DEBUTS ON C.B.S. IT'S BEEN ON EVER SINCE.

THE DEATH OF PRESIDENT EISENHOWER

March 28, 1969. Dwight David Eisenhower, thirty-ninth president of the United States, dies at Walter Reed Army Hospital in Washington, D.C., at seventy-eight after a long fight with coronary heart disease.

The joke was told years later of a man who had been asleep for twenty years. When he awakes, he asks to be brought up to date. "Well, first of all, Eisenhower is dead." The man responds, "Oh, my God! That means Nixon's president!"

CHAPPAQUIDDICK

July 18, 1969. U.S. Senator Edward Moore Kennedy (D-Mass.), known as Teddy, younger brother of President John and Senator Robert Kennedy, is driving near Chappaquiddick Island, Massachusetts, when his 1967 Oldsmobile Delmont 88 goes off the Dike Bridge and into Poucha Pond. His passenger is Mary Jo Kopechne, one of his staffers. She is stuck in the submerged car. Kennedy tries to save Kopechne, but he is unable to. She drowns. Although Kennedy speaks to his lawyers and the Kopechne family shortly after the accident, he does not inform police until ten hours after the incident. Kennedy later pleads guilty to leaving the scene of an accident after causing an injury and is sentenced to a two-month suspended jail term. He never fully recovers politically, although he is later reelected to the Senate for eight terms. Many believe that his actions and inactions at Chappaquiddick kept him from the White House.

In the early 1970s, some Nixon supporters drove around with bumper stickers on their cars proclaiming "Nobody died at the Watergate."

WOODSTOCK

August 15–18, 1969. Woodstock. Three days of music and rain on Max Yasgur's 600-acre farm in Bethel, New York, the biggest rock concert in history. Just the name Woodstock still evokes the 1960s.

The New York State Thruway closes after a twenty-mile traffic jam. The promoters decide to stop taking tickets—they make it a free concert. Among the performers: Jimi Hendrix, Arlo Guthrie, Crosby, Stills, Nash, and Young, Joe Cocker, Ten Years After, Joan Baez, The Band, Janis Joplin, Creedence Clearwater Revival, Sha-Na-Na, Johnny Winter, John Sebastian, Sly and the Family Stone, Santana, Jefferson Airplane, The Who, Country Joe and the Fish, Paul Butterfield Blues Band, and the Grateful Dead. Two deaths, two births. "Woodstock" joined the cultural lexicon almost immediately—"Were you at Woodstock?" It became one of those events like Don Larsen's perfect game in the 1956 World Series, or the Beatles concert at Shea Stadium. Some 12,000,000 people claimed to have been there. But there weren't quite that many—only half a million. Woodstock was the high-water mark for the counter-culture revolution of the 1960s.

CAN YOU TELL ME HOW TO GET TO SESAME STREET?

November 10, 1969. A new television program premiers on P.B.S. It's called Sesame Street. *Over the next thirty-seven-plus years, the show will record over 4,000 episodes. Jim Henson's Muppets— Kermit the Frog, Bert and Ernie, Grover, the Count, Oscar the Grouch, Big Bird, and Cookie Monster—all become household names and cultural icons.*

NO HAYNSWORTH, NO CARSWELL

November 22, 1969. Spiro Agnew, vice president of the United States, and president of the Senate, announces that the United State Senate had voted 45–55 not to confirm President Richard Nixon's nominee, Clement Haynsworth Jr. of South Carolina, to be an Associate Justice of the Supreme Court of the United States. Haynsworth, a federal circuit court judge, had ruled in cases involving corporations in which he owned stock. Haynsworth had also been accused of being antiunion and racist.

Haynsworth's rejection is the tenth time—and the first since 1930—the Senate has rejected a presidential nominee for the high Court.

Following Haynsworth's defeat, in a fit of pique, and believing that no matter how dreadful, the Senate would never reject *two* of his Supreme Court nominees in a row, President Richard Nixon—himself a lawyer—nominates an even worse disaster for the Court: G. Harrold Carswell.

Carswell had been a U.S. District Court judge and later a judge of the Federal Circuit Court for the Fifth Circuit.

On January 19, 1970, Nixon nominates Carswell to the Supreme Court of the United States. What probably contributes to Carswell's defeat in the Senate—besides his fifty-eight percent reversal rate—are the damning words of one of his most fervent supporters, United States Senator Roman Hruska, Republican of Nebraska: "Even if he is mediocre, there are a lot of mediocre judges and people and lawyers. They are entitled to a little representation, aren't they?"[4]

Carswell's nomination is defeated by the Senate on April 8, 1970 by a vote of 45–51.

Carswell later resigns as a federal judge. He runs for the Senate from Florida and loses. In 1976 he is arrested in a Florida mensroom and convicted of soliciting an undercover officer for sex.

Nixon eventually nominates Appeals Court Judge Harry Blackmun of Minnesota, a former lawyer for the Mayo Clinic, to the Supreme Court. Blackmun, while not a Southerner, is neither incompetent, unethical, racist, nor antiunion. Blackmun is confirmed by a vote of 94–0 and serves until 1994.

[4] No, they are not. The Supreme Court of the United States is not a place for mediocrities.

NO MORE CIGARETTE ADS ON T.V.

January 2, 1970. By act of Congress, the ban on cigarette ads on television goes into effect. The move costs the broadcast industry an estimated $220 million.

THE TRAGEDY OF KENT STATE

May 4, 1970. Four students are shot and killed by National Guardsmen during protests at Kent State University in Ohio. They are protesting the United States's illegal invasion of Cambodia.

After days of campus unrest, 1,000 Ohio National Guardsmen enter the campus of Kent State University to quell the unrest and put an end to non-violent antiwar demonstrations. The school prohibits the May 4 rally, but by noon there are 3,000 protesters. Across the Commons are about 1,000 Guardsmen with loaded M-1 rifles. A few minutes later, twenty-eight soldiers fire pistols and rifles. Most fire into the air or into the ground. But some of the soldiers fire directly at the students. Nearly seventy shots are fired in thirteen seconds.

Jeffrey Miller is shot in the mouth and killed. Allison Krause is shot in the left side of her body and killed in the parking lot, 330 feet from the Guardsmen. William Schroeder is shot in the back and killed while he, too, is in the parking lot, nearly 400 feet from the Guardsmen. A fourth student, Sandra Scheuer, is also shot and killed in the parking lot. Nine other students are wounded by military fire.

A photograph from Kent State that day shows fourteen-year-old Mary Vecchio, on one knee with arms outstretched, screaming over Jeffrey Miller's body as it lies supine on the ground. The photo wins the Pulitzer Prize for John Filto, at the time a photography major.

HATEFULNESS

February 20, 1971, 9:33 a.m. A message is sent, mistakenly telling the nation's T.V. and radio stations that the president of the United States had declared a national emergency, and that all normal broadcasting was to cease at once.

The message is an error, although the actual codeword used to trigger the alert—"hatefulness"—was in fact sent. A number of stations around the country go off the air, following the protocol when such a message, using the correct codeword, is received. A corrective message using the codeword "impish" is finally sent forty minutes later from the National Emergency Warning Center in Cheyenne Mountain, Colorado.

BYE, BYE, CHOO CHOO

April 30, 1971. The *Wabash Cannonball*, the legendary train from Detroit to St. Louis, makes its last run.

THE PENTAGON PAPERS CASE

June 13, 1971. *The New York Times* publishes the first installment of the Department of Defense's secret *History of U.S. Decision-Making Process on Viet Nam Policy*—The Pentagon Papers. (*The Times* is later joined by *The Washington Post* and *The Boston Globe* in publishing the document.) The United States government, through President Richard Nixon and Attorney General John Mitchell, bring suit to halt publication. Nixon seeks to determine who leaked the report. This is one of the first times in American history that the government seeks a "prior restraint" on newspaper publication. Nixon's henchmen burglarize the office of the psychiatrist of Daniel Ellsberg, who provided a photocopy of the report to the *Times*. The government's lawsuit is assigned, by lot, to Judge Murray Gurfein of the United States District Court for the Southern District of New York—*on his first day on the bench*. He denies an injunction, but orders a stay so the government may appeal his ruling.

The case is rushed to the Supreme Court of the United States. It is argued on June 26, 1971, and the court's decision is announced fourteen days later on June 30. The court votes six–three to uphold the First Amendment's ban on prior restraints, and permits the publication to continue.

Aside from embarrassing the government, nothing happens as a result of publication.

THE XXVITH AMENDMENT

July 1, 1971. The XXVIth Amendment to the Constitution of the United States, lowering the legal voting age to eighteen, is ratified. The idea that young men could be drafted at age eighteen, but could not vote until age twenty-one, led to the lowering of the voting age. Young women have never been subject to the draft.

THE HOWARD HUGHES HOAX

1971. One of the great hoaxes of the 20th century is perpetrated by Clifford Irving, an author. He claims to have interviewed the reclusive billionaire Howard Hughes. Hughes was an industrialist, philanthropist, aviator, and Hollywood film producer (among other things). He was also known as a recluse, living in a Las Vegas penthouse for years, without actual contact with the outside world. Many people thought he was dead.

Irving claims to have worked with Hughes on his autobiography. When Irving's veracity was questioned, Irving claims that he had the audio tapes to prove that he had really interviewed Hughes. Hughes is outraged by this fraudulent invasion of his privacy, and arranges an audio interview with, among other reporters, some who had known him well enough to recognize his voice. Hughes denies knowing Irving, or working with him on any book.

In 1972, Irving is convicted of fraud against his publisher and goes to federal prison for 14 months.

APOLLO 15

July 26–August 7, 1971. *Apollo 15.* The first car on the Moon, called the Lunar Roving Vehicle, drives 27.9 miles on the lunar surface. The astronauts are David Scott, Al Worden, and Jim Irwin.

D.D.T. BANNED

June 14, 1972. The Environmental Protection Agency bans the use of D.D.T. as a pesticide. The ban goes into effect at the end of the year.

> ## WATERGATE
>
> *June 17, 1972, 2:30 a.m. Five men are arrested burglarizing the offices of Larry O'Brien, the chairman of the Democratic National Committee in the Watergate Building in Washington, D.C. Ronald Ziegler, President Nixon's press secretary, calls it a "third-rate burglary." Perhaps so. But Nixon's days as president are numbered.*

GEORGE WALLACE SHOT

May 15, 1972. Former Alabama Governor George Wallace, a racist demagogue/populist, is running for president on the ticket of the American Independent Party. He is speaking to a campaign rally in Laurel, Maryland. Albert Bremer, a deranged suicidal loner dressed in red, white, and blue and sporting a "Wallace" button, shoots Wallace five times with a .38. Wallace survives. But he has been wounded in both arms, the stomach, and the intestines. Wallace spends the rest of his life in a wheelchair, paralyzed from the waist down.

The jury at Bremer's trial for attempted murder rejects his insanity defense. He is convicted and sentenced to sixty-three years in state prison.

THE [TEMPORARY] END OF THE DEATH PENALTY

June 29, 1972. In *Furman v. Georgia*, the Supreme Court of the United States rules five–four that the death penalty, as currently administered, is "cruel and unusual punishment," prohibited by the Eighth Amendment to the Constitution of the United States. As a result, 636 men and women on the nation's death rows have their sentences reduced to life imprisonment.

FIDDLER ON THE ROOF

July 2, 1972. After 3,242 performances—the most in Broadway musical history—*Fiddler on the Roof* closes. It's been running since it opened on September 22, 1964. The show, with a book by Joseph Stein, lyrics by Jerry Bock, and music by Sheldon Harnick, is a musical adaptation of the stories of Sholem Aleichem about Tevye, the milkman in czarist Russia with five daughters.

SILLY STRING DEBUTS

1972. Canned Silly String is introduced. In 2006, it finds a new and, apparently for the first time, useful purpose. American soldiers in Iraq use it to locate trip wires in booby-trapped buildings.

APOLLO 17

December 7–19, 1972. The last lunar mission is *Apollo 17,* the only one to take a geologist to the surface of the moon. Astronaut (and later New Mexico Senator) Harrison Schmitt brings back a record 249 pounds of moon rocks. Commander Eugene Cernan is the last man to walk on the moon, December 14, 1972.

ABORTIONS LEGALIZED

January 22, 1973. By a vote of seven–two in a case called Roe v. Wade, *the Supreme Court of the United States overturns laws that outlaw abortion in the first two trimesters of pregnancy.*

WATERGATE HEARINGS

May 18, 1973. A select committee of the United States Senate, chaired by Sam Ervin (D-N.C.), commences televised hearings into the Watergate affair. Sen. Ervin frequently calls himself "just an old country lawyer." Harvard Law School, class of 1922. On July 13, 1973, former Nixon assistant Alexander Butterfield testifies that Nixon recorded all telephone calls and conversations in the Oval Office. "NIXON BUGGED HIMSELF!" the headlines scream. On July 24, 1974, the Supreme Court of the United States unanimously rejects Nixon's claim of "executive privilege" and orders him to turn over sixty-four tapes to the Watergate Special Prosecutor.

I AM NOT A CROOK

November 18, 1973. Orlando, Florida. During a press-conference in the middle of the Watergate scandal and Agnew investigations, claiming that he had never profited from his government service as a congressman, senator, vice president, or president, beleaguered, embattled President Richard M. Nixon proclaims "[p]eople have got to know whether or not their President's a crook. Well, I am not a crook. I've earned everything I've got."

PUT YOUR MONEY WHERE YOUR TURKEY IS

Spiro "Ted" Agnew, born Spiro Theodore Anagnostopoulos, was the Republican governor of Maryland when he was selected by Richard M. Nixon as his running mate in 1968 and again in 1972. Before being elected governor in 1966, he had been the Baltimore County Executive. He carved out a staunchly conservative, "law and order" antimedia persona for himself, and as vice president he was known as "Nixon's Nixon," viciously and occasionally alliteratively attacking the administration's opponents. "Nattering nabobs of negativism" was one of his most memorable lines.

Agnew is charged with taking bribes as governor and as vice president, including accepting a turkey stuffed with cash from Maryland contractors and falsifying his tax returns. On October 10, 1973, he enters a "nolo contendere" plea in Federal Court in Baltimore. That is, while not specifically admitting his guilt, he does not contest the charges. Agnew resigns as vice president via a letter to Secretary of State Henry Kissinger— only the second vice president to resign. On December 28, 1832, John C. Calhoun was the first, because he had been elected to the Senate. Agnew is fined a paltry $10,000—about two turkeys' worth—disbarred as a lawyer, and placed on probation for three years. He is later sued privately and ordered to repay the state of Maryland $300,000.

In 1995, a bust of Agnew is unveiled in the Senate, near those of the other men who had served as vice president.

PATTY HEARST, URBAN GUERRILLA

February 1, 1974. Nineteen-year-old Patricia Hearst is the heir to the Hearst newspaper fortune. She is a student at the University of California at Berkeley when she is kidnapped—dragged out of her apartment and thrown in the trunk of a car—and held for ransom by something called the "Symbionese Liberation Army" (S.L.A.), whose leader is an escaped con named Donald DeFreeze. DeFreeze calls himself General Field Marshal Cinque Mtume. Hearst later says that she was locked in a closet for fifty-seven days, blindfolded, gagged, tied up, beaten, and raped. She also had to listen to S.L.A. propaganda drivel daily.

After her father pays the ransom by donating about $2 million in food to the poor, the kidnappers demand another $4 million. Her father balks—he doesn't have it. He offers to have his company put the money in escrow, payable upon Patty's release.

Patty Hearst says that she was then given a choice: 1. Be killed. Or 2. Join her captors. [Q#1: Hmmmm. Which would *you* choose?] She joins and changes her name to Tania.

On April 15, 1974, while armed with a rifle, Patricia Hearst helps her captors rob a Hibernia Bank in San Francisco, a heist that nets $10,000. Two people are shot during the holdup. [Q#2: If she is an unwilling participant, why doesn't she use the gun on her captors?]

On May 16, S.L.A. member Bill Harris was being held for shoplifting in a Los Angeles sporting goods store. In an effort to free him, Hearst sprays the store with gunfire. [Q#3: See Q #2, above.] She then takes out a second gun, and continues shooting.

She does not hit anybody. She and Harris escape in a van. But the police are able to trace a parking ticket left behind [she must have missed that lecture] and on May 17, the police find the S.L.A.'s hideout. There is a shootout, and the building bursts into flames. Six members of the S.L.A., including DeFreeze, are killed. But Patty Hearst is not there.

She is not arrested until September 18, 1975, when the F.B.I. finds her in San Francisco. She is charged with armed bank robbery and use of a firearm in the commission of a crime.

As she is being booked, she gives her occupation as "urban guerrilla."

Two years later, she comes to trial in Federal Court in San Francisco. Her lawyer, F. Lee Bailey, claims that she had been brainwashed by the S.L.A. Had she not participated in the crimes charged, he says, she would have been killed.

But she sits at the defense table wearing a paper ring that DeFreeze had given her. [Q#4: If she had been brainwashed, but was no longer under DeFreeze's spell, why not REMOVE THE RING?!?!?!?]

Patty Hearst is convicted on both charges and sentenced to seven years in federal prison. She entered a no-contest plea in the sporting goods store shootout.

In 1979, after two years in prison, President Carter commuted her sentence.

Now, she's in show business. She occasionally appears at celebrity roasts.

NIXON RESIGNS

August 8, 1974, 11:35 a.m. After 2,026 days in office, Richard Nixon resigns as president of the United States— the only president to resign in disgrace. Following protocol, Nixon actually resigns via a letter to Secretary of State Henry Kissinger.

"Dear Mr. Secretary: I hereby resign the office of President of the United States. Sincerely, Richard M. Nixon."[5]

Three articles of impeachment had been voted by the House Committee on the Judiciary, and there was a strong likelihood that the full House would vote to impeach Nixon.

At noon on August 9, while Nixon is flying into self-imposed exile at his home in San Clemente, California, Gerald Rudolph Ford (born Leslie Lynch King Jr.) is sworn in by Chief Justice Warren Burger as the thirty-eighth president of the United States.

In his "inaugural" speech, the new president reminds the country, "I am a Ford, not a Lincoln."

When he was facing a congressional committee determining his fitness to serve as vice president—after Agnew resigned—Ford was asked about pardoning Nixon. "The country wouldn't stand for it," he answered, which many equated with a promise not to issue a pardon. But on September 8, 1974, President Ford does just that. He grants Nixon an "absolute" pardon for any crime he committed or may have committed. Ford says that the country needs to heal from the years of Watergate angst and that any prosecution and trial for Nixon would have been divisive.

After Ford's succession to the presidency, his first important task, following the Twenty-Fifth Amendment, is to appoint a new vice president. He selects Nelson Aldrich Rockefeller, the former Republican governor of New York. Rockefeller had unsuccessfully sought the Republican nomination himself in 1964 and 1968. Rockefeller is confirmed by the Senate and then by the House on December 19, 1974, and is sworn in by Chief Justice Warren Burger that day, making Ford and Rockefeller the first unelected president and vice president in American history. But when Ford decides to seek a full four-year term in his own right in 1976, Rockefeller is not on the ticket. Ford's running mate is Senator Robert "Bob" Dole of Kansas, making the eight-letter Ford/Dole ticket one of the shortest-named in history. Although headline writers and campaign button makers rejoice, Ford and Dole lose to Jimmy Carter and Walter Mondale.

[5] Kissinger now has a fascinating and unique collection: Resignation letters from the vice president of the United States (Agnew), and from the president (Nixon).

HON. ELLA GRASSO

On November 5, 1974, Democrat Ella Grasso is elected Governor of Connecticut—the first woman elected governor in the United States in her own right, not succeeding a husband. Grasso is reelected in 1978 and serves through December 31, 1980, when she resigns for reasons of health. She dies on February 5, 1981.

THE ALASKA OIL PIPELINE

March 27, 1975. Construction begins on the Trans-Alaska oil pipeline, which will carry oil 800 miles south from Prudhoe Bay in the north to the ice-free port of Valdez. The first pipe is laid in the Tonsina River, near Valdez. The pipeline, the biggest private construction project in the nation's history, is completed on May 31, 1977. Nearly 22,000 workers are involved in the project.

FRANK ROBINSON—THE FIRST BLACK MANAGER

April 8, 1975. Frank Robinson becomes the first black manager in major league baseball, guiding the Cleveland Indians. Because he is a player-manager, he bats in the season's first game and homers.

DANGEROUS BUT INEPT

September 5, 1975. Lynette "Squeaky" Fromme, a follower of Charles Manson, tries to shoot President Gerald Ford. Her Colt .45 is loaded with four bullets, but fails to discharge. Ford is unhurt. *Saturday Night Live* later dubs Fromme "dangerous, but inept."

THE FIRST AMERICAN-BORN SAINT OF THE ROMAN CATHOLIC CHURCH

September 14, 1975. At the Vatican, Elizabeth Ann Seton is canonized—the first American-born saint of the Roman Catholic Church.

THE PET ROCK

April, 1975. The Pet Rock is invented (developed? created? marketed? hatched?) by Gary Dahl, a Californian advertising executive. The Pet Rock is sold in a box of excelsior with a care and feeding manual. At one point, Dahl sells 10,000 Pet Rocks per day for $3.95. Millions are sold before the fad passes. Nobody knows how many Pet Rocks are simply discarded or abandoned by their owners.

ANOTHER ATTEMPT ON THE LIFE OF PRESIDENT GERALD FORD

September 22, 1975. San Francisco. Seventeen days after Lynette (Squeaky) Fromme, a follower of Charles Manson, tries to kill President Gerald Ford, Sara Jane Moore tries, too, from forty feet away. Her gun, a .38, works. But she misses, because a bystander in the crowd grabs her arm and deflects the shot. Nobody is hurt.

Moore, an F.B.I. informant, was deeply troubled—*deeply troubled*—by the Patty Hearst case. She pleads guilty to attempted assassination and is sentenced to life in prison.

S.N.L.

October 11, 1975. A new program called *Saturday Night Live* airs 11:30 p.m.–1 a.m. on N.B.C. It stars the *Not Ready for Prime Time Players*, Gilda Radner, John Belushi, Chevy Chase, Dan Ackroyd, Garrett Morris, and Laraine Newman. The show features a different "guest host" every week. It is still on the air in 2006, thirty-one years later.

I'LL FRY TOMORROW

July 2, 1976. Four years after *Furman v. Georgia*, membership of the Supreme Court had changed. Now, in *Gregg v. Georgia*, the Court decides that capital punishment does not violate the Constitutional prohibition of "cruel and unusual punishment," and, following the Court's new guidelines, states are now free to hang, electrocute, gas, and shoot people again. On January 17, 1977, Gary Gilmore becomes the first man executed in the United States in a decade. He was convicted for a murder in Provo. Because he is convicted in Utah, he gets to choose the method of his own execution. Death by hanging or death by firing squad. (It's nice to have a choice!) He chooses the firing squad, and with the words "Let's do it," just after 8 a.m. he is legally shot to death in the prison yard in Salt Lake City. The firing squad consists of six riflemen (many had volunteered for the job) using Winchester Model 94 lever-action repeating rifles loaded with five Winchester Silver Tip 150-grain .30-30 caliber cartridges.

Firing squads traditionally have one more bullet than rifles, so each rifleman can go to sleep thinking "I had the blank."

I FOUGHT THE LAW AND THE LAW WON

June 22, 1977. John Mitchell, whose legal specialty was municipal bonds, and who was Richard Nixon's law partner, and a former Attorney General of the United States—the nation's chief law enforcement officer—goes to prison, to serve two to eight years for perjury, conspiracy, and obstruction of justice in the Watergate conspiracy. His sentence is later reduced. Says one law enforcement officer regarding Mitchell's arrest, "I just want to advise him of his rights."

ELVIS HAS LEFT THE BUILDING

August 17, 1977. Forty-two-year-old Elvis Presley, the "King of Rock 'n' Roll," dies of a heart attack in a bathroom at his palatial home "Graceland" in Memphis, Tennessee. Graceland remains open as a museum and a shrine. Presley's influence on the youth culture of America, and particularly on its music, is immeasurable. Presley sold over 500 million records.

Presley's television appearances were carefully doled out by his manager, Col. Tom Parker. Presley first appears on the popular *Ed Sullivan Show* on September 9, 1956—but only from the waist up. His gyrating hips were considered too sexually suggestive. If his millions of fans wanted to see the rest of him, they could pay to see him in his thirty-three films. His first was *Love Me Tender*.

When Presley is drafted into the U.S. Army, it is national news. A hit 1963 Broadway musical and later a film, *Bye Bye Birdie*, was loosely based on Presley going into the Army. He serves his eighteen-month hitch in Frieburg, West Germany, as a jeep driver.

Since his death, there have been hundreds of "Elvis sightings." Being an Elvis impersonator has become a fulltime job for hundreds of people. As one slogan puts it, "The United States had forty-three presidents, but just one King!"

THE ONLY WOMAN TO WIN THE MEDAL OF HONOR

June 10, 1977. President Jimmy Carter officially restores the Medal of Honor, which his predecessor Andrew Johnson had bestowed on Dr. Mary Edwards Walker, a physician with the Union Army. Her medal, along with about 900 others, was rescinded in 1917 by an army board, but she refused to return it and wore it for the rest of her life. Dr. Walker died in 1919. But Congress reversed the rescinding order, and posthumously restored her medal.

SEATTLE SLEW'S TRIPLE CROWN

Seattle Slew wins the Triple Crown of Thoroughbred Racing with jockey Jean Cruguet winning the Kentucky Derby, the Preakness, and on June 11, 1977, the Belmont Stakes.

ABSCAM

1978. The F.B.I. runs a sting[6] called A.B.S.C.A.M. to snare a number of public officials. The agents of "Abdul Enterprises, Ltd." offer money for favors—most of them taped. Convicted of bribery and conspiracy, disgraced, and imprisoned were U.S. Senator Harrison Williams (D-N.J.—three years in prison plus censure by the Senate), Rep. Richard Kelly (R-Florida—thirteen months), John Jenrette (D-S.C.—two years in prison. In 1989, Jenrette got thirty days for stealing a necktie from a department store), Raymond Lederer (D-Penna.—three years), Michael "Ozzie" Myers (D-Penna.—expelled by a House vote, the first since 1861, of 376–30, plus three years in prison), and Frank Thompson (D-N.J.—three years). John M. Murphy (D-N.Y.), a West Point graduate, does not testify at his trial. He is convicted of a lesser charge and sentenced to three years in prison. Angelo Errichetti, the major of Camden, New Jersey, is also convicted and sent to federal prison.

---

[6] Frequently but redundantly called a "sting operation." See other redundancies such as "free pass," "S.A.L.T. Talks," "shower activity," or "A.T.M. Machine."

REV. JIM JONES AND JONESTOWN

November 18, 1978. Jim Jones had been a streetcorner preacher with degrees from Indiana University and Butler University. He founded his People's Temple in Indianapolis in 1956. Jones was ordained as a minister of the Disciples of Christ in 1964. In 1965, he moved his ministry to Ukiah in Northern California. Jones was a respected community leader—he served on the San Francisco Housing Authority— but he craved more privacy for his followers, and by 1977 the People's Temple had moved to a 4,000-acre compound in Guyana, where he thought they'd be free from prying eyes.

Once in Guyana, his paranoia and megalomania became more evident. He claimed to be the incarnation of Jesus, Ikhnaton, Buddah, Father Divine, and Lenin.

U.S. Congressman Leo Ryan (D-Calif.), accompanied by reporters, visits Jonestown to investigate alleged abuse. Jones wants People's Temple counsel Mark Lane (author of *Rush to Judgment*, a bestseller that attacked the methods and conclusions of the Warren Commission) to be present. After a day in Jonestown, Ryan tries to leave with four cult members who have had enough. Jones fears what would happen to Jonestown if word of his activities got back to the United States, so he orders Ryan killed. Ryan is killed. His aides James Schollaert and Jackie Speier are wounded. Four cult members and three reporters are shot and killed at the Port Kiatuma airport. Eleven are wounded.

At 5 p.m. local time at the "People's Temple," Jones and 913 of his followers, including Americans, kill themselves—the disciples by drinking Kool-Aid poisoned with cyanide, Valium, Penegram, and chloral hydrate, an act they had rehearsed with Jones—one of the worst mass suicides in history. Of the dead, 276 are children. Jones shoots himself in the head.

Y'ALL READY FOR THIS?

October 3, 1979. Pope John Paul II celebrates mass at Madison Square Garden in New York City for 19,000 ebullient teenagers. The pontiff enters the Garden to the music from *Battlestar Galactica* and *Rocky* played by the 100-piece St. Francis High School Band.

The Holy Father is cheered to hear: "Rack 'em up, stack 'em up, bust 'em in two. Holy Father, we're for you!"

THE XIIITH WINTER OLYMPICS IN LAKE PLACID, NEW YORK

February 14, 1980. Vice President Walter Mondale opens the XIIIth Winter Olympic Games in Lake Placid, New York. These games have two highlights. Speedskater Eric Heiden, wearing a skin-tight hooded gold lamé body suit, wins five gold medals—a feat never duplicated—and sets five world records.

But there is another highlight, one for the ages—"The Miracle On Ice." An American team of college hockey players, coached by Herb Brooks (the last man cut from the American hockey team that won a gold medal in the 1960 Olympics at Squaw Valley), beats the vaunted Soviet team four–three and then the Finns four–two in the gold medal game.

March 21, 1980. Reacting to the December 24, 1979 Soviet invasion of Afghanistan, President Jimmy Carter issues an ultimatum: if the Soviets do not withdraw from Afghanistan by 12:01 a.m. on February 20, 1980, the United States will boycott the 1980 Summer Olympics, to be held in Moscow. The Soviet troops stay, and by a two–one vote the U.S. Olympic Committee supports the president and votes not to send a team to Moscow. The official announcement is issued on March 21, 1980. Hundreds of American athletes who have trained for years for this one showcase event are denied the opportunity to compete. N.B.C.'s coverage of the games is severely limited.

China, Japan, Canada, West Germany, and over fifty other countries follow the American lead and boycott the Moscow games. But others, such as Great Britain and Italy, do not.

In retaliation, the Soviets decide not to attend the 1984 games in Los Angeles, citing "security" problems.

ROSIE RUIZ

April 21, 1980. Despite looking fresh, not sweaty, and not particularly out of breath, amateur runner Rosie Ruiz, who had been training for only eighteen months and was unknown in running circles, is crowned as the winner of the eighty-fourth Boston Marathon. She beats Jackie Gareau of Canada, who had led for the last half of the race, in record time: 2 hours, 31 minutes, 56 seconds, the third-fastest marathon ever. Gareau's time: 2:34:28.

But nobody had heard of Ruiz, a twenty-six-year-old from New York. Moreover, nobody recalled seeing her during the race. And she did not appear in any of the thousands of photos of the race, which were examined, except for the last half-mile.

A week later, although she maintained her innocence, Ruiz is stripped of her title. She refuses to return her medal. Gareau is declared the winner after all. Ruiz is also disqualified from the New York Marathon, which she "ran" weeks before to qualify for the Boston race. Witnesses claim to have spoken with Ruiz on the subway at the time of the race.

Ruiz's name has entered the language, synonymous with hoaxes, trickery, and cheating, especially in athletic events.

SHE'S GONNA BLOW!

May 18, 1980, 8:32 a.m. An earthquake—5.1 on the Richter scale—shakes Mt. St. Helens, ninety miles south of Seattle. Part of the mountain's north face collapses and a mushroom cloud of smoke and ash rises for miles. Nearly 230 square miles of forest is destroyed by the blast or buried under volcanic ash. The eruption lasts for over nine hours.

WHO SHOT J.R.?

November 21, 1980. The "Who Shot J.R.?" episode of *Dallas* becomes the most watched T.V. show in history, so far. It is seen by 90 million viewers.

I HEARD THE NEWS TODAY

December 8, 1980. Forty-year-old former Beatle John Lennon is shot and killed by Mark David Chapman in front of the Dakota, Lennon's apartment house in New York City. Lennon's death shocks the country and the world. Chapman, who claims that he heard voices telling him to kill Lennon, pleads guilty and is sentenced to life in prison.

P.A.T.C.O.

August 5, 1981. President Ronald Reagan, former president of the Sceen Actors Guild, and the only former union president to be President of the United States, fires 11,359 striking air traffic controllers. The union is eventually decertified. Reagan notes that the air traffic controllers, members of P.A.T.C.O. (Professional Air Traffic Controllers Organization), all took a solemn oath never to strike against the United States. Some are quick to remind Mr. Reagan that in 1940 he took a solemn oath to stay married to Jane Wyman until "death do us part." Reagan and Wyman divorced in 1948.

NO LONGER "THE BRETHREN"

July 7, 1981. President Ronald Reagan nominates Sandra Day O'Connor of Arizona to succeed Potter Stewart on the Supreme Court of the United States—the first woman to join "The Brethren." O'Connor is confirmed by a unanimous Senate, September 22, 1981, and serves until 2006.

A BAD WAY TO IMPRESS JODIE FOSTER

March 30, 1981. In an effort to impress actress Jodie Foster, John Hinckley—who had read Mark David Chapman's published diary about his shooting of John Lennon—fires six shots from his .22 Rohm RG-14 handgun at President Ronald Reagan on a street in Washington, D.C. Reagan is shot in the chest and rushed to St. Elizabeth's hospital, where, just before emergency surgery, he tells his doctor, "I hope you're a Republican." Reagan makes a full recovery.

Secret Service agent Tim McCarthy is shot in the right chest, trying to block a bullet meant for Reagan. Washington, D.C., police officer Thomas Delahanty is also hit.

Widely respected Presidential Press Secretary James Brady is shot in the head and suffers a debilitating brain injury, but recovers sufficiently to become a champion of gun control laws.[7]

Secretary of State Alexander Haig is roundly criticized as something of a megalomaniac for saying, at a hastily-called White House briefing, "I'm in charge here." As Secretary of State, Haig was fourth in line for the presidency (after the vice president, the speaker of the House, and the president *pro tem* of the Senate). And as the senior Cabinet officer— and in the absence of Vice President George H.W. Bush, who was out of town—Haig *was* in charge, i.e., the senior government official on the scene.

Hinckley goes to trial in Washington, D.C., for attempted murder and related charges. The full might of the federal government is brought to bear at his trial. But on June 21, 1982 the jury finds Hinckley not guilty by reason of insanity. Asked for his comment, Hinckley's lawyer Vincent Fuller issues one of the great legal quotes of all time: "Another day, another dollar."

[7] Although he is unable to return to his job, Brady remains the Presidential Press Secretary for the remainder of Reagan's presidency—at least in title. Other spokesmen are always "acting" or "deputy" press secretaries, a sign of respect for Brady.

TIME TO RETIRE. REALLY. I MEAN IT. TODAY.

January 19, 1982. At the insistence of seventy-one-year-old President Ronald Reagan, eighty-two-year-old Admiral Hyman Rickover, the "father of the nuclear Navy"—the Navy's longest serving officer—retires after sixty-four years of service

THE TYLENOL MURDERS

1982–1986. Tylenol capsules laced with cyanide are planted in stores in and around Chicago. Seven people die as a result of taking the poisoned pills. The crime has never been solved, and the $100,000 reward offered by Johnson & Johnson, Tylenol's manufacturer, remains unclaimed.

As a result of this mysterious crime, a new industry is born, almost instantly: safety, tamper-evident sealing.

BIGFOOT

November 26, 1982. Only after 84-year-old Ray Wallace dies on November 26, 2002 does his family reveal that there is no "Bigfoot," or "Sasquatch," the mythical giant ape-man of the Pacific Northwest. All the footprints, films, and sightings were fake—done by Wallace. In one, Wallace's wife Elna put on a gorilla suit and was filmed by Roger Patterson. Many were taken in by the hoax.

SEE SALLY RIDE. SEE SALLY RIDE IN SPACE

JUNE 18–24, 1983. SALLY RIDE BECOMES THE FIRST AMERICAN WOMAN IN SPACE, ON THE SHUTTLE *CHALLENGER*.

GOODBYE, FAREWELL, AND AMEN

February 28, 1983. The $2^1/_2$-hour final episode of "M*A*S*H" attracts an audience of 106 million viewers, the largest ever.

AMERICA LOSES THE AMERICA'S CUP

September 27, 1983. For the first time since its inception in 1851, the America's Cup yacht race is won by a country not called "The United States." Australia wins the race off Newport, Rhode Island, by twenty-five seconds. The next race, in 1987, will be held in Perth, Australia.

MARTIN LUTHER KING JR.'S BIRTHDAY BECOMES A HOLIDAY

November 2, 1983. President Ronald Reagan signs into law a bill making Martin Luther King Jr.'s birthday a national holiday. It is now celebrated on the third Monday in January.

THE XXIIIRD OLYMPICS IN LOS ANGELES

July 28, 1984. President Ronald Reagan, a Californian, officially opens the XXIIIrd Olympics in Los Angeles, California.

Mary Lou Retton captures the hearts of millions by winning the gold medal in the all-around (the first American to do so), a silver in the vault, and bronze medals in the floor exercise and the uneven bars. She also wins a silver team medal.

Edwin Moses wins the gold medal in the 400-meter hurdles—part of a string of 122 consecutive victories.

But the undisputed star of the 1984 games is Carl Lewis, who matches his idol Jesse Owens by wining four gold medals (he won nine medals overall in his stellar Olympic career): the 100 meters, 200 meters, 4 x 100 meters, and the long jump.

THE FIRST WOMAN CHIEF

December 14, 1985. For the first time in American history, a Native American tribe—in this case, the Cherokees—chooses a woman, Wilma Mankiller, as its chief.

THE SHUTTLE CHALLENGER EXPLODES

January 28, 1986. Christa McAuliffe, a high school teacher from Concord, New Hampshire, was going to be the first teacher in space. She trained for 114 hours with the astronauts in Houston and at Cape Kennedy in Florida. She was going to be the one to help explain space, weightlessness, and all that astronauts do to American schoolchildren. Televisions were set up in many classrooms to watch her take off on the tenth flight of the space shuttle *Challenger*.

Unfortunately, 73 seconds after liftoff, *Challenger* explodes eleven miles high and nine miles downrange of Cape Kennedy. All seven crew members—McAuliffe, Francis Scobee, Judith Resnik, Elison Onizuka, Michael Smith, Ron McNair, and Gregory Jarvis—are killed.

DON'T GET BORKED

July 1, 1987. President Ronald Reagan nominates Robert Bork to the Supreme Court of the United States. As Solicitor General on October 20, 1973, it was Bork who carried out Nixon's orders and fired Watergate Special Prosecutor Archibald Cox after Attorney General Elliot Richardson and Deputy Attorney General William Ruckelshaus resigned rather than fire Cox. Bork was thus the Acting Attorney General.

In far-ranging confirmation hearings, Bork discusses his judicial philosophy with members of the Senate Judiciary Committee, expounding on his disagreement with one person–one vote, his beliefs that there is no general right to privacy (and therefore no right to an abortion), and that the poll tax is not necessarily unconstitutional. Bork expresses his view that forced school prayer is a good idea, and he criticizes a court decision striking down restrictive covenants based on race.

On October 23, 1987, Bork's nomination to the Court is defeated in the Senate by a vote of forty-two to fifty-eight. Subsequent nominees have been advised to keep their comments to the Judiciary Committee short and simple, and to avoid discussing any issues that might come before the court lest they be "Borked."

ONE GIANT LEAP

February 2, 1989. Bill White, former first baseman for the Giants, Cardinals, and Phillies, and the first black broadcaster (February 10, 1971), is named president of the National League. He is the first black man to hold such a high position in sports.

THE EXXON VALDEZ OIL SPILL

March 24, 1989. The oil tanker *Exxon Valdez* spills more than 11 million gallons of crude oil in Alaska's pristine Prince William Sound—the largest oil spill in American history. The spill endangers commercial fishing as well as ten million birds, whales, sea lions, sea otters, and harbor porpoises. Many animals die. The ship's name was ultimately changed to *SeaRiver Mediterranean*. Instead of spending more money to clean up the mess, Exxon pays for a new advertising campaign, patting itself on the back for helping clean up the mess.

THE LOMA PRIETA EARTHQUAKE

October 17, 1989, 5:04 p.m., Pacific Coast Time. An earthquake, measured at 6.9 on the Richter scale, strikes. Its epicenter is in Loma Prieta, ten miles northeast of Santa Cruz, California. The earthquake is captured on live television, as Game 3 of the World Series is about to begin in San Francisco's Candlestick Park. The Series is postponed for ten days. The quake kills sixty-two people.

NIXON IMPEACHED!

Question: Was Nixon impeached? Answer: Yes! After his conviction by jury trial on a charge of perjury, U.S. District Court Judge Walter sentences Nixon to six years and ten months in federal prison. Later, he is impeached by the House of Representatives. On November 3, 1989, he is convicted by the Senate vote and removed from office.

THE FIRST BLACK GOVERNOR

January 13, 1990. Douglas Wilder takes the oath of office as the sixty-sixth Governor of Virginia—the first black man elected governor in American history. The second is Deval L. Patrick, elected Governor of Massachusetts in 2006.

THE SIMPSONS

December 17, 1989. *The Simpsons* makes its debut on the FOX network as a half-hour show. The characters first came to life as thirty-second fillers on *The Tracey Ullman Show*, April 19, 1987. After over seventeen years, it is the longest-running animated program ever, and the longest-running comedy of all time. It may surpass *Gunsmoke*'s twenty-year record for the longest-running show of all time. *The Simpsons* has won a Peabody Award, over twenty Emmys, and the Simpsons family has a star on the Hollywood Walk of Fame.

AYE-AYE, CAPTAIN

DECEMBER 28, 1990. FOR THE FIRST TIME IN HISTORY, A WOMAN—COMMANDER DARLENE ISKRA—IS THE CAPTAIN OF A U.S. NAVY SHIP, THE APTLY NAMED SALVAGE VESSEL U.S.S. *OPPORTUNE*.

CLARENCE THOMAS AND ANITA HILL

July 8, 1991. President George H. W. Bush nominates Clarence Thomas of Georgia to succeed Thurgood Marshall as an Associate Justice of the Supreme Court of the United States. Thomas, an ultra-conservative African-American judge of the U.S. Circuit Court of Appeals for the D.C. Circuit, is an opponent of Affirmative Action. How conservative is Thomas?

His nomination is opposed by the N.A.A.C.P., the National Bar Association, and the Urban League. *That* conservative.

Thomas faces intense questioning by the Senate Judiciary Committee in September. He testifies that he has no opinion on the divisive national question of abortion. The Judiciary Committee vote on his nomination ends in a seven–seven tie, and his name is sent to the full Senate without recommendation and is set for a full vote on his confirmation.

But the Judiciary Committee decides to reopen its hearings when Anita Hill, a professor of law at the University of Oklahoma, levels explicit and detailed sexual harassment charges against Thomas. She claims that he harassed her sexually when they worked together for two years at the Equal Employment Opportunity Commission, which Thomas chaired.

Around 40 million American households are mesmerized by the televised hearings October 11–13, 1991. Hill and Thomas both testify. They cannot both be telling the truth. Thomas says that Hill's charges amount to "a high-tech lynching for uppity Blacks."

Vice President Dick Cheney is standing by in case of a tie vote. But the Senate votes to confirm Thomas by a vote of 52–48. He takes his seat as a Justice of the Supreme Court—a lifetime appointment—on October 23, 1991.

While the hearings and vote end in Thomas's accession to the High Court, they serve a different purpose by putting sexual harassment on the national agenda.

JEFFREY DAHMER

February 15, 1992. Jeffrey Dahmer is convicted of fifteen counts of murder in Milwaukee, Wisconsin. He tried to turn many of his victims into "zombies," for him to use as sex toys. He drilled holes in their heads, then poured caustic liquids in the holes.

At his trial, Dahmer pleads guilty but insane, but the jury finds him sane. Wisconsin does not have a death penalty, so Dahmer is sentenced to fifteen consecutive life sentences—936 years in prison. He is killed in prison on November 28, 1994, with 934 years left on his sentence.

HURRICANE ANDREW

August 24, 1992. Hurricane Andrew, a Category 4 storm, with winds up to 175 miles per hour, hits southeast Florida on its way to Louisiana. At the time, Andrew is the worst natural disaster to strike the United States. Some 700,000 people are evacuated, but many of them don't go very far. Five days after the storm, in the largest domestic military operation in peacetime, 23,000 troops land at what had been Homestead Air Force base. The base is wiped out, not to be reopened for two years.

The city of Homestead is devastated, too. The storm takes forty lives. The damage is estimated at $30 billion; 250,000 are left homeless; 100,000 south Floridians leave, never to return.

THEEEEEEEEERE'S JOHNNY!

MAY 22, 1992. JOHNNY CARSON'S LAST PROGRAM AS HOST OF N.B.C.'S *Tonight Show*. HE IS SUCCEEDED (NOT REPLACED) BY JAY LENO.

THE BOMBING OF THE WORLD TRADE CENTER

February 26, 1993. Ramzi Yousef and Omar Abdel-Rahman mastermind the bombing of the World Trade Center in New York, which kills six people and injures over 1,000. Yousef, Abdel-Rahman, and eight others are convicted and sentenced to nearly 250 years in prison.

JANET RENO

March 12, 1993. Janet Reno becomes the first woman to serve as Attorney General of the United States. She serves until the end of the Clinton administration, January 20, 2003.

TAKE YOUR DAUGHTERS TO WORK

April 28, 1993. It's the first "Take Your Daughters to Work Day" sponsored by the M.S. Foundation.

THE NORTHRIDGE EARTHQUAKE

January 17, 1994, 4:35.55 a.m., Pacific Standard Time. An earthquake measured at 6.7 on the Richter scale hits southern California, centered in Northridge. It is one of the rare earthquakes to hit a city. Fifty-one people are killed and 9,000 seriously injured. Damage is felt as far as eighty-five miles away.

SPY SCANDAL

February 24, 1994. Aldrich Ames, who has been a top official at the C.I.A. for thirty-one years, specializing in the K.G.B. and other aspects of Soviet intelligence, is arrested by the F.B.I. in Arlington, Virginia, and charged with spying for the Russians. What a co-ink-ee-dink! A number of American operatives were murdered as a result of Ames's treachery. His wife Rosario is arrested as an accomplice. Both plead guilty in one of the worst security lapses in American history. Ames is sentenced to life without parole. Rosario gets sixty-three months in prison.

I DON'T GO POGO

May 10, 1994. After fourteen years on death row, John Wayne Gacey is put to death in Illinois' Joliet State Prison. Gacey, one of the country's most prolific serial killers, used to entertain neighborhood children as "Pogo the Clown." Gacey is said to have killed at least thirty-three victims, including twenty-nine buried in the crawl space under his house.

THE O.J. SIMPSON CASE

June 17, 1994. Orenthal James Simpson is arrested and charged with the June 12 murder of his ex-wife Nicole and her companion Ronald Goldman. Simpson had been a college football star at the University of Southern California and in the National Football League. He went on to a career doing commercials (Hertz) and in films (*The Towering Inferno, The Naked Gun 2^1/$_2$: The Smell of Fear, The Naked Gun 33^1/$_3$: The Final Insult*) and television (*Ironside, Medical Center*). Simpson remains incarcerated for fifteen months.

A jury is selected in November, 1994. Simpson is represented by lawyers dubbed "The Dream Team": Johnnie Cochrane, F. Lee Bailey, Alan Dershowitz, Barry Scheck, and Robert Shapiro.

On October 3, 1995, Simpson is acquitted. But he is later found liable in a civil trial and ordered to pay $8.5 million to the Brown and Goldman families. His home and his 1968 Heisman Trophy are auctioned off to pay part of his debt.

Today, he spends his time looking for the real killers on the fourteenth tee. He has not paid one cent.

Simpson's actions, of course, will make it hard for *all* the kids named Orenthal.

THE YEAR WITHOUT A WORLD SERIES

September 14, 1994. The World Series is canceled by baseball commissioner Bud Selig for the first time since 1904. The players are on strike.

THE BOMBING OF THE ALBERT P. MURRAH BUILDING

April 19, 1995. The Albert P. Murrah[8] Building in Oklahoma City is bombed and 168 people are killed. Although early speculation about the perpetrator focused on foreign terrorists, the man who made the bomb (with others) and planted it is Timothy McVeigh, a veteran of the United States Army, and winner of the Bronze Star. He was upset and mad at the federal government for, among other things, the February 29, 1993 raid on David Koresh (true name Vernon Howell) and his cult followers, the Branch Dividians, in Waco Texas. The Bureau of Alcohol, Tobacco, and Firearms and the F.B.I. entered the Waco compound by force, but their building caught fire. Koresh and eighty-one of his followers were killed.

McVeigh is tried and convicted. All of his appeals are turned down. His death on June 11, 2001, is the first federal execution by lethal injection. It is carried out at the Federal prison in Terre Haute, Indiana, and is viewed on closed-circuit television by 232 survivors and family members.

---

[8] The building was named for a federal judge who was an Oklahoma native.

MOTHER TERESA

IN 1995, MOTHER TERESA OF CALCUTTA BECOMES AN
HONORARY CITIZEN OF THE UNITED STATES JUST
EIGHT YEARS BEFORE SHE WAS BEATIFIED.

THE XXVITH OLYMPICS IN ATLANTA, 1996

*July 19, 1996. President Bill Clinton opens the XXVIth
Olympics in Atlanta, Georgia. The torch is lit by
Muhammad Ali, who won the gold medal as a light
heavyweight in Rome in 1960, when he was known as
Cassius Marcellus Clay. Atlanta's Centennial Olympic
Park is bombed on July 27, killing Alice Hawthorne, a
Georgia woman, and Robert Sanderson, an off-duty
Birmingham, Alabama, police officer. Nurse Emily Lyons
loses the use of an eye. One hundred others are injured.*

*Eric Rudolph, who had been living in the mountains of
North Carolina as a fugitive for some time, is arrested on
May 31, 2003 and charged with the crime. He pleads
guilty on April 13, 2005 and is sentenced to three
consecutive life sentences.*

MADAM SECRETARY

January 23, 1997. Madeleine Albright, born Marie Jana Korbelová in Prague, becomes the first female Secretary of State.

THE UNABOMBER

January 22, 1998. Theodore Kaczynski, a Harvard graduate, went off the proverbial deep end. On this date, he pleads guilty to conducting a reign of terror on the United States. Between May 25, 1978, with his first bomb in Chicago, and April 24, 1995, when one of his bombs killed a lobbyist for the timber industry, he sent/planted fifteen bombs to further his eco-anarchist views, and his hatred of the industrial world. He targeted an advertising executive, an airline pilot, a medical researcher, and a computer expert. His bombs killed three people and injured twenty-three. He thought that these targets isolated people from nature and from each other. He wound up living in a shack in Montana.

In September, 1995, the Unabomber promises to halt his reign of terror if newspapers throughout the country print what comes to be known as his 35,000-word manifesto: "Industrial Society and Its Future." Clearly, although Kaczynski was a bright, educated man, these are the ravings of a lunatic. His brother David recognizes the thoughts and rantings of his brother, and after some soul-searching, David Kaczynski calls the F.B.I. and fingers his brother. Ted Kaczynski is arrested on April 3, 1996.

Denied the right to represent himself, Kaczynski pleads guilty to thirteen counts, including the three fatal bombings. He is sentenced to life imprisonment without the possibility of parole.

62 THEN 70 IN '98

September 8, 1998. Mark McGwire of the St. Louis Cardinals breaks Roger Maris's record by hitting his sixty-second home run of the season. McGwire climbs into the stands to hug Maris's family. McGwire goes on to hit seventy homers in 1998.

Uncertain Times

2000–2007

"'Tis the star-spangled banner;
O long may it wave
O'er the land of the free,
and the home of the brave!"

Francis Scott Key, 1814

WHAT HAPPENED?

January 1, 2000. First day of the new millennium. Nothing happens. Warehouses remain full of remaindered books predicting the end of the world, the crash of thousands of computers, stuck elevators, crashing of planes, stalled trains, stuck drawbridges, floods, fires, tsunamis, etc. Nothing.

MARCH ON COLUMBIA

January 17, 2000. 46,000 protestors converge on South Carolina's state capitol to protest a flag—the Confederate Battle Flag, flying over the state capitol.

HONORED AT LAST

June 21, 2000. Fifty-five years after World War II ended, twenty-one Asian-American heroes of that conflict are honored at the White House, as President Clinton bestows upon them the nation's highest honor for military bravery—the Medal of Honor. Some had previously been given the Distinguished Service Cross, but were denied the nation's highest honor because of their race. Only five are still alive to receive their new medals—including Daniel K. Inouye, United States Senator from Hawaii.

WHAT A MESS!

OCTOBER 11, 2000. A DAM COLLAPSES NEAR INEZ, KENTUCKY. OVER 300 MILLION GALLONS OF COAL SLURRY SLUDGE ARE RELEASED OVER 100 MILES OF STREAMS, TRIBUTARIES OF THE BIG SANDY RIVER'S TUG FORK. MILLIONS OF FISH ARE KILLED IN ONE OF THE WORST ENVIRONMENTAL DISASTERS IN HISTORY.

FROM FIRST LADY TO 1 OF 100

November 7, 2000. Hillary Rodham Clinton, wife of president William Jefferson "Bill" Clinton, is overwhelmingly elected to the United States Senate from New York—the first "First Lady" elected to the Senate or any office.

HOW NOT TO SELECT A PRESIDENT

December 12, 2000. Forty days after Election Day, George Bush is selected president of the United States after a much disputed race, when the Supreme Court, in a seven–two vote, rules in *Bush v. Gore* that all of the votes in Florida (where *Bush's brother Jeb is the governor*) did *not* have to be counted. Bush gets all of Florida's twenty-seven electoral votes and thus comes out ahead, with 271 electoral votes to Vice President Albert Gore's 266. But Gore wins more popular votes.

THE ATTACKS ON THE WORLD TRADE CENTER, THE PENTAGON, AND PENNSYLVANIA

September 11, 2001. One of those days like April 12, 1945—the day F.D.R. died—October 3, 1951—the day of Bobby Thomson's pennant-winning home run—and November 22, 1963, the day John F. Kennedy was murdered. The question: "Where were you when ____?"

Another one of those cataclysmic dates was September 11, 2001. It becomes known as "Nine Eleven." And "Nine Eleven" becomes a shorthand way of referring to any act of terrorism. "It's another Nine Eleven." Or, "We don't need another Nine Eleven."

On that date, nineteen terrorists armed with plastic knives take over four American flights. The first two are American Airlines Flight 11, a Boeing 767-223ER with eighty-one passengers and a crew of 11 from Boston to Los Angeles, and United Airlines Flight 175, a Boeing 767-222, also from Boston to Los Angeles (and therefore both full of fuel). The first crashes into the North Tower of New York's World Trade Center at 8:45 a.m., exploding and killing all on board. The second plane crashes into the South Tower and explodes at 9:03 a.m., also killing all on board. Both buildings are engulfed in flames. The South Tower collapses at 10:05 a.m. At 10:28 a.m., the North Tower collapses.

The death toll at the World Trade Center is 2,973. Among the dead are 343 New York City firefighters, 23

New York City Police officers, 37 Port Authority Police officers, and three Uniformed Court Officers, who had run over from the nearby New York State courthouses to help.

At about the same time, terrorists divert two other planes: At 9:43 a.m. American Airlines Flight 77, a Boeing 757-223 from Washington to Los Angeles with fifty-eight passengers and a crew of six, crashes into the Pentagon in Arlington, Virginia, killing 125.

Finally, United Airlines Flight 93, a Boeing 757-200 from Newark, New Jersey, to San Francisco, with thirty-eight passengers and a crew of seven, is diverted, probably to fly into the White House. But many believe passengers interfered with the terrorists' plans and the plane crashes into a pasture in Shankville, Pennsylvania. All forty-six on board are killed.

The attacks of September 11, 2001, the worst terrorist events in the nation's history, kill more people than the Japanese surprise attack on Pearl Harbor on December 7, 1941.

In the days that follow, the attacks are traced to Al Qaeda, an Islamist terrorist group. The United States invades Afghanistan, searching for Al Qaeda leader Osama Bin-Laden. A reward of $25,000,000 is posted for him. Afghanistan's rulers, fundamentalist Islamists known as the Taliban, are ousted, and a new, ostensibly pro-American democratic government is elected.

GOING, GOING, GONE
October 7, 2001. Barry Bonds of the San
Francisco Giants hits his record seventy-third home
run of the season.

THE SHUTTLE *COLUMBIA* EXPLODES

February 1, 2002. The space shuttle *Columbia* explodes over Texas fifteen minutes before it is scheduled to land, after a successful sixteen-day mission. Astronauts Rick Husband, William McCool, Michael Anderson, David Brown—a former stilt walker in the circus—Kalpana Chawla, Laurel Clark, and Ilan Ramon—Israel's first astronaut—are all killed.

NANCY PELOSI

November 14, 2002. Nancy Pelosi of California is elected Democratic Leader of the U.S. House of Representatives. She is the first woman to hold such a leadership position of either party.
She takes office on January 7, 2003. After the Democratic victories in the 2006 off-year elections, in 2007 Pelosi becomes Speaker of the House—the first woman to hold such a high office in the United States.

THE FIRST SIT-DOWN DEMONSTRATION

JANUARY, 2003. THE MONTGOMERY MUNICIPAL BUS, ON WHICH ROSA PARKS REFUSED TO MOVE TO THE SEGREGATED BACK, IS RESTORED AND DISPLAYED AT THE HENRY FORD MUSEUM IN DEARBORN, MICHIGAN.

LIVE FREE OR DIE

May 3, 2003. The Old Man of the Mountain, a New Hampshire icon—the state symbol, it was on the commemorative New Hampshire quarter—collapses and disappears on May 3, 2003. Between 2,000 and 10,000 years old, the stone outcropping was 40 feet tall and 25 feet wide, and stood out on Profile Mountain near Franconia Notch.

FIRST PRESIDENTIAL NOVEL

November 11, 2003. *The Hornet's Nest*, by Jimmy Carter, a novel of the Revolutionary War, is published. It's the first novel ever published by a future, current, former, or ex-president of the United States.

CAN YOU BELIEVE IT?

October 27, 2004. Bedlam in Boston and throughout New England and "Red Sox Nation" as the Boston Red Sox sweep the St. Louis Cardinals to win the World Series for the first time since 1918. In the now immortal words of Red Sox broadcaster Joe Castiglione, "Can you believe it?"

NATIONAL MUSEUM OF THE AMERICAN INDIAN

2004. The National Museum of the American Indian opens on the Mall in Washington, D.C. One of 16 buildings which are part of the Smithsonian, it is established by Act of Congress.

KATRINA

August 29, 2005. Florida, Alabama, Louisiana, and Mississippi, as well as oil platforms in the Gulf of Mexico, are hit hard by Hurricane Katrina, a Category 5 storm (the strongest: winds over 170 mph), the worst natural disaster ever to hit the United States. Katrina's swath covers 90,000 square miles, and is felt as far north as Canada. Katrina drops five inches of rain on a large part of southeastern Florida. Some areas get fifteen inches. Other areas get as much as one inch per hour. Nearly two million people are without electricity.

Katrina is followed on September 24 by Rita and, on October 24, Wilma, another Category 5 monster storm.

Some 28,000 National Guard troops are used in the Katrina recovery efforts.

Katrina leaves over 1,000 dead in its wake, and causes two billion dollars worth of damage in Florida alone. In Louisiana, a million people are without electricity, 800,000 are homeless, and eighty percent of New Orleans is flooded, some parts under twenty feet of water. Four levees had been breached. The airport is flooded and closed.

In Mississippi, 236 are dead and ninety percent of the buildings on the coastline are wiped out.

In Mississippi and Louisiana, many people wait on what was left of their roofs to be rescued by helicopter.

In Alabama, nearly 600,000 people were without electricity. Price gouging and panic lead some gas stations to ask six dollars for a gallon of gas.

Many of the evacuees go to Texas—at least a quarter million—until the governor said that the state could not absorb any more, and begged neighboring states to accept some.

The Federal Emergency Management Agency (F.E.M.A.) is very slow (i.e., glacial) to respond to the hurricane, and although President George W. Bush gives F.E.M.A. director Michael Brown a vote of confidence ("Brownie, you're doing a heck of a job"), Brownie resigns on September 12. Apparently, his previous job supervising judges and stewards at the International Arabian Horse Association for eleven years— from which he was fired—had not given him the background needed to get ice, food, trailers, and medicine to evacuees, or to coordinate post-disaster relief. Who'd have thought?

Many refugees are temporarily housed at Houston's Astrodome, no longer used since the Astros moved to Minute Maid Park (formerly Enron Field) on April 7, 2000. When Barbara Bush, the wife of ex-president George H. W. Bush and the mother of President George W. Bush, arrives for a visit, she says: "What I'm hearing, which is sort of scary, is they all want to stay in Texas. Everyone is so overwhelmed by the hospitality. And so many of the people in the arena here, you know, were underprivileged anyway, so this is working very well for them."

RITA

On September 21, 2005, Hurricane Rita does not cause as much property damage or take as many lives as Katrina—probably because so many had already been evacuated. Rita is responsible for sixty-two deaths and nearly $17 billion of destruction in the U.S. alone.

Former president Bill Clinton and ex-president George H. W. Bush put aside their partisan differences and join to start the Bush/Clinton Katrina Fund to raise private funds to help Katrina survivors.

SOME PEOPLE HAVE TOO MUCH FREE TIME DEPT.

2006. Jim Doyle, the governor of Wisconsin, claims to have seen each episode of *Seinfeld* at least eight times. At the governor's annual Christmas party in the Governor's Mansion in Madison, he proudly displays his Festivus Pole.

> *MAKE ROOM FOR DADDY*
> *October 17, 2006. According to the Census Bureau, the population of the United States has risen to 300 million people.*

IT'S A WIN WIN SITUATION

November 7, 2006. In the midterm elections, Democrats win enough seats to take over the House of Representatives and the U.S. Senate. In fact, incumbent Democrats do not lose a single race for governor, senator, or representative.

GOOD YUNTIV

December 10, 2006. For the first time, a menorah, marking the eight days of Chanukah, the Jewish Festival of Lights, is lit in the White House (on the second night of the Holiday.) President George W. Bush and his wife Laura Bush are present when the "White House Menorah" is lit.

Index